MATCH STICKS

MATCH STICKS

AN EDUCATION IN BLACK AND WHITE

FRED ENGH
WITH JANN SEAL

SQUAREONE
PUBLISHERS

Cover Designer: Jeannie Rosado
In-House Editor: Erica Shur
Typesetter: Gary A. Rosenberg
Front Cover Matchsticks Artist: Dan Engh
Back Cover Photographer: Kathi Rodgers

Square One Publishers
115 Herricks Road
Garden City Park, NY 11040
(516) 535-2010 • (877) 900-BOOK
www.squareonepublishers.com

Library of Congress Cataloging-in-Publication Data
Names: Engh, Fred, author. | Seal, Jann, author.
Title: Matchsticks : an education in black and white / Fred Engh with Jann Seal.
Description: Garden City Park, NY : Square One Publishers, 2021.
Identifiers: LCCN 2020038622 (print) | LCCN 2020038623 (ebook) | ISBN
    9780757005053 (hardback) | ISBN 9780757055058 (epub)
Subjects: LCSH: Engh, Fred. | United States—Race relations—History—20th
    century. | Maryland State College—History. | Teachers—United
    States—Biography.
Classification: LCC LA2317.E528 A3 2021 (print) | LCC LA2317.E528 (ebook)
    | DDC 370.92 [B]—dc23
LC record available at https://lccn.loc.gov/2020038622
LC ebook record available at https://lccn.loc.gov/2020038623

Printed in India

10   9   8   7   6   5   4   3   2   1

Contents

To Joanna and Bob

Acknowledgments

There are many people I would like to thank for being there both throughout my life as well as helping me put this story together. First are some of the people who made a difference in my life early on. Mrs. Kelly. Strangely enough, Mrs. Kelly, my fifth grade teacher, instilled in me the love of sports. As a fifth grader she let our class play dodgeball almost weekly throughout the year. I discovered through dodgeball what sports were all about, speed, reflexes, lateral movement, and challenging yourself to never give up. I loved that about sports and all that followed. And to Burt Raughley, who introduced me to the game of golf. Our seemingly endless hours on the driving range and golf courses embedded in me a love for the game that still exists

To Dr. Charles Tippetts. I was fortunate enough to be able to go to Mercersburg Academy, an exclusive prep school in Pennsylvania. My mother found a way to get me enrolled. I worked for my keep by working in the dining room morning, noon, and night. Because of a learning disorder, I could barely keep up with my grades. Dr. Tippetts threatened to expel me, but at the last minute changed his mind. I am forever grateful. Without his decision to let me stay, I would never have graduated from high school and certainly not be able to write this book.

To Dr William Hytche. This man, my math teacher, at Maryland State turned my life around with his teaching skills. He made me understand learning against all odds. To Pop Watson. How could I not recognize Pop for, first, making that all-important announcement on the radio that set me on my course. And second, for being the outstanding PE teacher and head of the PE department at Maryland State.

To Father Paul Fink. How often I have said throughout my life that had Father Fink not recommended me for the coaching job in Wilmington, Delaware, my life would have taken a far different turn. Oh, how I wish he were still alive to thank. To Father Francis Burns. The principal at St. Elizabeth High School, who agreed to hire me as the head football coach. He took a big chance hiring someone who had little to zero experience as a football coach. Thank goodness I proved him right.

To Don Bushore, the executive Director of the Athletic Institute in Chicago. It was Don who gave me my first opportunity in the "big" world of sports. He allowed me to do my own thing as he appointed me as the Director of Youth Sports. That opportunity opened the door to me achieving my life ambition to encourage leaders of sports and to make sports positive, safe, and fun for children around the world.

To Bob Spanjian, Dick Spanjian , Fred Brooks, and Bob Seagren. All top people in the sporting goods industry. Without the belief from these four fine people, I might have never made it. With a wife and seven children, I was struggling to make my dream come true. I was at "the end of my rope." No money left to build a dream. Only one hope. These four men would believe in my dream and, in the very beginning, contributed the financial aid to make it happen. How can you acknowledge them enough?

Then there are those who helped provide me with the guidance and encouragement to move forward with this work. To Pat Duff, my sister-in law. My wife, Mike, and Pat had just returned from the movie, *Green Book*. Pat couldn't wait to say, "Fred, this movie is your story in reverse. You should write a book about your experience going to an all-Black college." In truth, it was far from my own story, but it got me thinking about the lessons I came away with from that experience. To Chauncey and Mary Taylor. My two friends who know firsthand the meaning of racism. They offered their unique perspective on the direction for this book. As Chauncey said, "Don't be afraid to tell it as it is." To Dan Engh, my nephew, whose artistic talent seems endless. His artwork for the cover of this book won me over from day one.

To Jann Seal. For being able to share the journey of finishing this work with skill, caring, and humor. And to Rudy Shur. I thought I knew how to write a book, but apparently I had a lot to learn, and it turned out that Rudy was a good teacher. I'm grateful that he saw me through this endeavor. To Jeri and Dona Yates. I'm lumping these two together because they read the manuscript as it progressed and offered their opinions. Thankfully, they were positive. To my sister-in-law Mary Jo, who gave me the encouragement to tell my story. To Ron Russo. When you are involved in creating the most important book of your life, you need someone to tell you what you need to hear . . . not what you want to hear. Once I got the okay from Ron, I knew we were on the right path.

And then, of course, is my family. To my wife Mike. All one would have to do to know the role she played in the story that this book tells, is to read it. As my friend Ron Russo said, "She must be a saint." And she is. I would be remiss if I didn't name every one of our seven kids who were around to see the result of how my experience of going to Maryland State College turned out. Here they are in chronological order: Kathi, David, Eric, John, Darin, Joanna, and Pat. I would also be remiss if I didn't mention the final editing my daughter Joanna did for the book.

And finally, to Muzzie, Coolie, brothers Lynn, Rohn, and Denis. And to sisters Dona and Mary Joel. A family who shaped everyone's life.

Preface

In a time when the Black Lives Matter movement truly matters, why on earth would a white guy write a book about his experiences becoming the first white student to receive his diploma at an all-Black college in 1961? Or the first white student to participate in sports at the same Black college. Crazy white guy? I hope not. This book is not about any problems I had breaking the color barrier, in reverse. It's not about the dangers I faced riding in a car with four Black teammates on our way to golf matches. And it's not about my taking an active role in protests in the Sixties. Instead, this book is simply about my education at Maryland State College on the Eastern Shore of Maryland—and one all-too-short friendship. The education I received may have put me on the right path, but it was that friendship that allowed me to see beyond the color of someone's skin.

I was raised at a time when overt racism was practically everywhere. I thought it was normal. I didn't think I was doing anything different than any of my white friends or family. And while I had no animosity against African Americans, I just accepted it as being the way it was. It was only when I began classes at Maryland State to earn a degree in Physical Education that I learned the truth about myself. Accepting the status quo was just as bad as any overt act of hatred. That lesson has stayed with me all these years

There is no doubt in my mind that the non-profit organization that I founded and ran for over thirty years—the National Alliance for Youth Sports (NAYS)—was influenced by my time at Maryland State. As a father and physical education teacher, I understood how the way you raise your children and what you teach your students can greatly impact how they see others. NAYS was designed to make organized sports fun for children and to try to level the playing field for all children, no matter what color or ethnicity they are. These lessons of acceptance should not have come from a college experience as they did for me, but they did.

In the 1960s, we saw an uprising of Black activists from across this country demand equal rights. In 2020, we once again see a new movement of both Blacks, and now many whites, demanding the same rights as well as equal justice. While sixty years have passed since the Sixties, too many of our generation never learned the meaning of tolerance. And while I have never been vocal in my approach, I believe that the colorblindness we need begins with our young generations.

A few years back, I had written a book called *Why Johnny Hates Sports*. It was and still is published by Square One Publishers. Over the years, I have become friends with the publisher there, Rudy Shur. During a conversation, I had mentioned that I happened to have attended an all-Black college. I also mentioned the honor I was paid by the college a few years ago for my work with NAYS and the book I had written. From that point on, he would not stop asking me questions about my experiences at Maryland State College. About an hour or so into his questioning, he said, "Fred, this is your next book. Put together a manuscript, and let's get it out there."

Writing a book about one's life is a little more challenging than writing about what's bad in organized sports for children. I needed some help. Having been the CEO of an organization for over thirty years, I have hired and fired my share of "would-be" professionals. One thing I found—if you have a sense of humor, are willing to work hard, and be loyal to the cause, then you are my kind of person. I found that kind of person in Jann Seal. Beyond the basics, she had the experience, the talent, and the appreciation for the story. Right from the beginning, we worked together like good friends, never letting egos get in the way. This work is a reflection of a most enjoyable collaboration.

There are a few things I would like to mention in regard to writing this book. First, we have changed just a handful of names. Most of the of names used are true-to-life. Second, in the 1960s, the vast majority of time the word "negro" or "colored person" was used to describe an African American or affiliated organization such as a "Negro College." Except for a few incidents in which these words were used to reflect the racial disparity of the times, I have chosen to use the words "Blacks" and "African Americans." And third, epithets such as the N-word, were also commonly used, and I am afraid, still are. I hate that word, as I told my publisher. Instead, I have only used it three times in the book as "n - - - - r."

In making sure that I had the facts accurate, I looked back at the many events that took place during the various timelines in my story. What I found were many newsworthy items that reflected both the racial injustices and achievements of those times. While these events may not be part of my own life's story, they should not in fact be overlooked. So to put my own story in context, I have included timelines to the years 1941, 1961, 1962, 1963, 2012, and 2020 throughout this book.

In closing, I am more than aware that we live in a time of change. Division seems to be running rampant. If you are in one political party, you hate the other. If you are poor, you hate the rich. If you are rich, you consider yourself superior to the poor. If you are white, you seem to have a wide variety of groups to hate. These feelings are so easily passed on to our children—and it gets us nowhere. The story in this book, again, is about an education and a friendship, and how anyone can change for the better given the right environment.

1
Back to Campus

It was late afternoon, and I wasn't due at the awards ceremony for a few hours. I wanted to get to the campus early, alone, to walk around—just me and my memories. It had been many years since I had been to the school, and I needed the time to travel in my mind from the 1960s till now. The school had been named Maryland State College when I had attended, a cozy little hamlet of a campus that rested along the banks of the Manokin River. Today, my alma mater is called the University of Maryland Eastern Shore.

Located in the small town of Princess Anne, on Maryland's eastern shore, the college had been established in 1886. Then called Delaware Conference Academy, it had started off with a mere eight students. Yet for the generation of the many students who followed, this school represented an opportunity that could take them out of a life of hardship and poverty. It could afford them the means to make a living wage for themselves and their families. And by the time I attended, it was obvious that the importance of the school's history had not been lost on the student body. They respected the education and opportunities the college offered. In the 1960s, when racial demonstrations on college campuses dominated the news across the country, the students at Maryland State set the tone for what was to be expected on their campus. Nothing was to disrupt this chance for a higher education. Its history was not lost on me, but for now, however, I just wanted to walk the campus, I needed time to figure out why I hadn't returned to the place that strengthened my backbone and gave me my career focus.

Time had changed many things.

As I strolled through the campus, admiring the Georgian architecture and all the new buildings that had gone up between my student days and the present, I saw a sign pointing me to a driving range. That alone showed me how much things had changed, and I had to see for myself where today's students practiced their golf skills.

A cold February gust played with my hair as I stood at the edge of the driving range, a recent addition to the University of Maryland Eastern Shore's athletic facilities and the pride of its newly named golf program, the Golf Academy. The athletic department had come a long way since my teammates and I lugged our hand-me-down golf clubs to compete with other schools across the region. We weren't the Golf Academy then, just a bunch of guys who loved the game and wanted to play.

As I looked out at the manicured grass and tufts of fresh turf, I laughed to myself, thinking back to when the golf team I played on was relegated to practicing on one of the most rundown golf courses in Maryland. We called it a "goat ranch" because of the scrub and sand lining the fairways, tees, and greens. The Winter Quarters golf course in the nearby town of Pocomoke fit the description perfectly. Why anyone would pay to whack balls there was beyond my imagination. But with no real alternatives close by, that's where we practiced.

I stood there with what I imagine was a distant, empty stare on my face, as a wave of sadness crossed my thoughts. The college had closed the golf program soon after our banner season, and it took forty-three years for the University of Maryland Eastern Shore to bring the game back to the school. I was in the right place at the right time, as far as golf and the college were concerned. I also remembered what it took for me to convince my wife what being on the golf team meant. While I knew it would take me away from our family time together, I explained that it would make a great addition to my physical education resume. But I knew it would also allow me to play the game I loved—for free.

The butterflies in my stomach were in full flight as I approached the theatre arts building. My wife, Michaele—Mike, as everyone called her—had been on this long journey with me, ever since I convinced her to marry a guy with no obvious future. No education, as it were. And someone who had a dream, but no measurable way to achieve it. She was on her way to the campus, traveling by car along with four of our now-grown children as I took this solitary walk into the past; they would be in the audience for me that evening. My other three kids wanted to be there, but they all lived out of state. Mike promised to take a lot of pictures, though, and to send them copies. It's not easy arranging the lives of grown children. Mike, the kids who were with us, and I had arranged to meet after the ceremony for a special celebration. Until that time, I would be out of reach, onstage, as one of the honorees.

"Are you Mister Engh?" the young lady asked when greeting me at the door, mistaking the pronunciation of my last name by calling me Mister "Eng-ah." Such is life when your last name is a four-letter word comprised almost entirely of consonants.

She took my arm and escorted me backstage, where several other honorees were milling about. Through a small opening in the closed, maroon curtain, I could see bright, shining lights and heard the clamor of excitement as a sea of well-wishers seated at tables in the audience waited anxiously for the presentations to begin. In accepting the invitation, I hadn't really thought too much about how attending this event would affect me. But now, I felt really nervous.

I was being inducted into the college's popular and well-regarded Hall of Fame—not for any academic achievement, mind you, but because of my years of commitment to youth sports and the non-profit organization I had established. Sports entered my life because I was athletic, not academic. I had trouble reading because of a learning disorder that had yet to be discovered. Until high school, I was never considered for first string on any sports team. I had a small build, wore ratty shoes, and probably looked more like a future claims adjuster than a star athlete.

Still, sports lit a fire in me—an ardent flame all too often extinguished by coaches whose only goal was winning. It seemed they cared less about the mindset of kids who wanted to play just for the sheer fun and enjoyment of sports. Years later, I wrote a book about why many kids hate sports and was soon thereafter named one of America's top sports educators for calling attention to the problem. It was for those achievements that I was being inducted this evening. Then again it may have also been for being the first white student to participate in sports at what in the 1960s was a Black college, or for being the first white student to walk across this same stage to receive his diploma. I was thrilled either way.

All those years earlier, I had come to Maryland State College as a "nobody." My future looked bleak. I now returned a "somebody"—and as I peeked out from backstage at the ocean of black faces in the audience, I realized that the education I had received at this then-Black college was what helped put me on this stage. This school, and the lessons I learned here, had given me the grounding that set me on my life's remarkable path.

My only regret was that Bob Taylor—my golfing teammate, my rock in a sea of pebbles, and my first true friend here at this school—wasn't there alongside me. I could hear his soft Southern voice taunting me: *Damn, Engh! About time your lily-white ass was up here getting inducted for something. I always knew white boys were slow, but man, you make the Maryland Terrapin look fast.*

I chuckled upon hearing the sound of his rich, baritone voice in my head. After all, it had been Bob who had led me through some of the most turbulent and frightening years of my life. Nearly from the moment I first walked through the school's front gates, he had taken the young guy that I once had been—with no direction—and helped to make him into a better man. Before that, though, it was my mother, Muzzie, who had scared the hell out of me and shook

4

me to my core with an especially harsh serving of cutting words. Bob may have had my back during my Maryland State College days, but it was my mother who unintentionally put me on that campus in the first place.

1941 TIMELINE

February 13, 1941. Private Felix Hall—a Black U.S. soldier stationed at Fort Benning in Georgia—was reported missing, but no search was undertaken. A month after he disappeared, a training Army company found Private Hall's body, still in uniform, at the bottom of a ravine, with a rope tied around his neck. His hands and feet were bound with haywire. While initially the Army asserted that the death was a suicide, it eventually revised its assessment and acknowledged that Hall was killed. Hall's killers were never identified.

March 19, 1941. After much political lobbying by the NAACP, the Army began training the first all-Black flying unit initially called the 99th Pursuit Squadron and then renamed the 99th Fighter Squadron. The men in this group, nicknamed the Tuskegee Airmen, were trained as a separate unit from the rest of the Army trainees, and fought in North Africa, Sicily and Italy during World War II. While a small step forward, the U.S. Army continued to keep its fighting forces segregated.

April 28, 1941. The U.S. Supreme Court unanimously ruled that under the 1887 Interstate Commerce Act, African Americans were entitled to equal passenger accommodations on the nation's railroads. Prior to this decision, railroad companies whose trains traveled through states with segregation laws had to abide by these state laws.

June, 25, 1941. In response to Black civil rights leader A. Philip Randolph's threat of a massive "March on Washington" demanding a fair share of jobs and an end to segregation in government departments and the Armed Forces, President Roosevelt issued an executive order banning discrimination in defense jobs a day before the march was scheduled to occur. The Federal government, however, would not challenge any existing state or local discrimination laws or practices. Twenty-two years later, on August 28,1963, Randolph delivered on his "March on Washington" project in which Martin Luther King, Jr. delivered his "I Have a Dream" speech.

November 21, 1941. In Watson v. Stone, the Florida Supreme Court overturned the gun conviction of a white man carrying a gun without a license. Justice Rivers Buford wrote in his concurring opinion: "The Act was passed for the purpose of disarming negro laborers. . . . [It] was never intended to be applied to the white population and in practice has never been so applied."

December 7, 1941. At 8 A.M., Sunday morning, Japanese fighter planes carried out an attack on the U.S. naval base on Pearl Harbor. More than 2,400 Americans were killed and 1,000 people were wounded. The next day, President Franklin Roosevelt went in front of a joint session of Congress to ask for a declaration of war. Within an hour of his seven-minute "Infamy Speech," the declaration was passed, and the United States had formally entered World War Two.

December 11, 1941. Five days after the bombing of Pearl Harbor, Sylvia Tucker, an African-American mother, visited her local Red Cross Center in Detroit to donate blood for our servicemen. When she arrived at the center, the supervisor turned her away telling her "Orders from the National Offices barred Negro blood donors at this time."

2

The Long Road

was six years old in June 1941 when the long arm of the Great Depression reached into the 1940s. That, and the fear of an impending war drained my parents' pockets and forced my family to leave our spacious home in the affluent section of Johnstown, Pennsylvania. My mother had come from a family of wealth. Suddenly, she was being downsized into a world she had never known. Muzzie, that was our name for my mother and none of us had any idea where it came from. Even my dad had a strange nickname—Coolie—another family mystery. But Muzzie was tormented, distraught, and lost. The thought of leaving all she knew and heading off into the great unknown seemed to unsettle her deeply. My father had lost his job as an insurance salesman, owed money to the wrong people, and debt collectors were ringing our doorbell all hours of the day and night. Coolie needed to get out of town, fast. One night after dinner, he told my mother and the five of us kids that we were going to have to move away and live somewhere else. We sat, all of us in shock, as he tried to give us reasons for the move—but his words didn't mask the helplessness we felt.

The walls of our house weren't thick enough to muffle the arguments that came from my parents' room during that night and into the morning. "We can't do this," my mother cried. My father's stern reply was always the same: "Either you and the kids come with me, or I'm going by myself. You decide."

I laid in my bed, pulling the covers up over my head, and tried hard not to cry. Sleep didn't come easily that night.

My older brother, Lynn, was beside himself. What kid, just going into high school, wants to leave his pals, his school, his sports teams? Everything he had known all his life was being taken away from him, and he'd have to start all over again. He spent the next day whining, begging, crying monster tears until Muzzie couldn't take it anymore.

With Lynn at her side the whole time, my mother had a long conversation with her sister, Mary Lenore. It was agreed that Lynn would stay with her and her family in Johnstown until other arrangements could be made. Lynn's face during that phone call told the rest of us all we needed to know about what was being said. His tears dried up and he started jumping up and down hugging Muzzie. Lynn was a happy boy. The rest of us? Not so much.

That night, Muzzie pulled all of us close to her and started telling us the story of why we needed to move. She struggled with the words, but I remember her saying that we had to go somewhere closer to the ocean—that the ocean air and seashore was what the doctor said was good for her health. A child's mind doesn't always put two and two together in the grown-up world, but Muzzie had a hard time looking any of us in the eye as she told her story and when she finished, she simply stood up and walked out of the room. We kids looked at each other with a million questions written on our faces—the biggest one, of course, had to do with our mother's health, as none of us ever remembered Muzzie being sick.

The next day, a large truck pulled up in front of our house and big, burly men started loading our furniture onto it. My brother Rohn and sisters Dona and Mary Joel stood next to me on the curb watching in horror as our treasures went from our house into the truck. "Where are they taking our stuff, Coolie?" I asked, bewildered, as the men loaded our brand-new refrigerator into the belly of the truck. He didn't answer. My father was a man both troubled and in trouble. We didn't know it at the time, but we'd never see our furniture again. We learned only later that Coolie had sold the furniture so we would have enough money to keep us housed and fed.

The truck pulled away, and it was like waving good-bye to all we knew in life. What belongings we had left were stuffed into suitcases and loaded into our car. Maude, our housekeeper, came out of the empty house and stood on the sidewalk, tears running down her face. Her chubby arms wrapped themselves around me and pulled me so close it was hard to breathe. I was her special boy, her "baby," and was going out of her life, perhaps forever.

While Muzzie and Coolie wrapped Lynn in their arms, hugging and kissing and sharing their sad good-byes, the rest of us kids piled into the car. There were two front seats, and the back was barely wide enough to hold the rest of us. Wiping tears from her face, Muzzie got into the car, pulling me with her and holding me close as she insisted I share the front seat with her. That's the price you pay for being the smallest.

It was late afternoon as Coolie put the family car in reverse and backed out of the driveway, and we couldn't help but look over our shoulders to wave good-bye to our empty house. As we reached the two-lane highway leading out of Johnstown, the mountainous terrain of western Pennsylvania dissolved into a flat Maryland countryside filled with newly planted vegetable crops of the summer. Cornfields stretched as far as the eye could see, and Black corn pickers labored in the hot sun, slowly stuffing the ripened ears into baskets.

The six of us had little space in which to move around in the car. Later in the trip, I was ordered to sit in the back seat, which was already stuffed with Rohn and my sisters. Crowding me in, even though I was the smallest of them all, didn't work, and they pushed me up to the space under the rear window. It was surprisingly comfortable, and I could look up and see the cloud formations and the figures that they seemed to resemble. Faces, snow cones, butterflies—all kinds of shapes floated in my mind as we motored along. I was snoozing in my car-loft when a new smell awakened me—a scent that I would regard fondly for the rest of my life. Misty ocean air, blowing in the wind. Stretching out in the distance was water as far as the eye could see—all the way to the horizon. We kids dropped our jaws in amazement at what we were seeing. The car windows were rolled down, and my siblings began to poke their heads out—screaming all the while at the sights, sounds, and smell of ocean air. It was as if we were on a magical flying carpet as we rode into the town of Ocean City, Maryland.

Coolie pulled off the highway and parked the car in front of the wooden boardwalk. Full of excitement and looking like children running out of school at the end of the term, we jumped from the car and raced across the white sand toward the ocean ahead. Never had we seen or imagined such a spectacular sight. The waves of the ocean pounded on our ankles as we giggled and screamed as children do. Sometimes, big waves would splash us up to our waist with Muzzie yelling in anger for us not to get wet.

After the excitement wore off, we dried ourselves in the heat of the lingering sun, then returned to the car where Muzzie handed us our dinner—bologna sandwiches on white bread. Heaven! Coolie was busy marching up and down the streets of the town, looking for some place for us to live, while summer vacationers were packing up for the day and lugging sand chairs, beach towels, and toys as they headed off the beach at the end of their day.

Muzzie tried to warn us that finding a place to live would not be easy, since there were so many of us. After all, it was the beginning of the summer season, and we couldn't afford much. Yet, when Coolie came back to the car with a smile on his face, we knew he'd found us a place to live.

Wooden houses lined the street on which we now drove, all with front porches and some with garages tucked into the side. Coolie pulled our car up in front of one house, and we all jumped out and started running up the stairs to what we thought was our new home. Coolie stopped us and pointed instead to the adjacent garage. *That* was our new home? Muzzie shivered, shrugged her shoulders, and marched into our one-room garage apartment with us kids trailing behind.

That first night in our garage apartment gave new meaning to the term "roughing it." We slept in our clothes on the cement floor, ate more bologna sandwiches, and had to wait until Coolie returned from the local grocery store with toilet paper before we could use the bathroom. Muzzie used up her tissues to wipe the tears and runny noses all of us had as we adjusted to our new home.

The next day dawned sunny and bright, and we peered out the garage door to see other moms and dads marching toward the beach with their kids and beach paraphernalia in tow. We spent the day shopping for mattresses, household goods, and food. Finally, when all was deposited into the apartment, Muzzie told us to get our bathing suits on. There was still time to enjoy the sun and sand.

We adjusted to the garage-home, and eventually looked at it as a kind of adventure. Muzzie did her best cooking on a two-burner range with just a pot or two, and my sisters learned how to make pancakes and even biscuits in our tiny kitchen. The good part of having a kitchen that was only three feet square, as we came to learn, was that you didn't have to move around much. Everything was at your fingertips—and it took less time to clean up after meals. The card table that was left in the apartment became our dining table, and Muzzie even found a nice tablecloth, at the second-hand store in town.

There were few windows in the apartment to let the sea breezes in, and on those hot and muggy Maryland summer days, we were all left fighting for any fresh air that passed our way. The beach became our salvation. It helped my older siblings get over their remorse at having to leave friends, but for me, I was on an adventure. I was just happy to be an almost six-year-old who lived in paradise.

My siblings and I would play in the surf all day—then we would go back to our garage-house, take quick showers to save on hot water, and put pajamas on over our increasingly tanned bodies while Muzzie figured out what to feed us. Sometimes I would find her in the tiny kitchen, sniffling and wiping her eyes and nose on her shirt sleeve. She would always blame it on chopping onions—even when there weren't any onions in sight.

Coolie frequently disappeared from Ocean City after we got settled, traveling around, looking for whatever work he could find. He would check in by calling the phone booth near our apartment on a specific day and time. We all crowded in and around the booth just to say "Hi" to him, and then waited outside while he and Muzzie said a few words. I once overheard her begging Coolie to take us back to Johnstown. A few months in the apartment was okay, she figured, but she thought that we would all go nuts once the fall season came and we weren't able to go outdoors as much. She said that she would rather live in a garage in Johnstown, where she *knew* people, than be stranded in Ocean City—where she didn't know a soul. For my mother, these calls with Coolie always ended the same way: She would breathe in deeply, exhale slowly, and force a reassuring smile before joining us again out on the sidewalk. One thing I can say about my mother: She was always a devout Catholic, and a believer. I still remember how she would tell us kids that "With prayer, things will work out." And usually they did—one way or another.

Our days would often begin when we threw open the front door, which allowed a rush of fresh ocean breezes to flow through the cramped apartment. Idyllic as these days often were, maintaining a sense of harmony within the family was always a challenge. The closeness caused a few fights among us kids and Muzzie knew we needed to get out of our packed sardine can early in the morning if we were going to survive the bruises. Her solution for avoiding our own World War from breaking out in our living/dining/sleeping quarters was to pack a lunch, grab some towels, and cart us off to the beach. It became a pleasant routine, and I often thought about how joyful that first summer in Ocean City was, in spite of the living conditions. With Coolie away for what seemed to be most of the summer, it was just my mother Muzzie, my brother, my two sisters, and me, all sharing that one-room space. With sunny days and warm nights, what else could we ask for?

We spent that summer on the Eastern Shore, doing what most kids do. We built forts along the shoreline. My older brother, Rohn, and I would roll up newspapers and make telescopes and scour the horizon looking for U-boats moving in offshore. Early one morning we even thought we spied one and ran swiftly to the policeman who was then patrolling the beachfront, yelling frantically that we were about to be invaded. He appeased us for a few minutes, even taking our newspaper telescopes to see for himself. Shaking his head, he let us know that what we saw was a fishing boat, not an enemy submarine.

Ocean City had a few big grocery stores, in addition to the fast-food markets; and whenever Muzzie got an envelope marked "GENERAL DELIVERY" from Coolie, she would treat us to "good" food that would last for at least one or two meals. She would put on a nice dress, clean us up, and we would parade to the shop for food, with the promise of one sweet treat each if we stayed together and behaved. We must have been a real sight! Four ragamuffins and a lady who still had class, in spite of her circumstances. We were an easy target of conversation, and it wasn't lost on one elderly lady shopping in the same aisle.

We noticed her immediately as she wheeled her grocery cart full of steak, chicken, the greenest of vegetables, and two gallons of ice cream toward us. Muzzie sized the lady up quickly as she approached. To her surprise, though, the lady stopped us and kindly said, "I'm amazed at how you can handle so many well-behaved children. Whatever you're doing, you're doing it right!" The two women started talking, as my siblings and I just about drooled over those two gallons of ice cream. When the lady asked where we lived, Muzzie could only say, "Temporary accommodation."

Most people liked our mother as soon as they met her. So I guess that's why Mrs. Barton felt compelled to walk over to our umbrella one day while we were on the beach and introduce herself again, reminding her of that first meeting they had had in the grocery store. Little did my mother know, as she looked up to see the formidable Mrs. Barton standing under her fringed umbrella, that the woman was someone who would soon come to change our lives forever. Or at least for a few years.

During the next few weeks of summer, when Mrs. Barton returned to Ocean City from her home in Baltimore, she would invite my mother to lunch at her spacious oceanfront home, a few feet away from the beach. There they would discuss each other's life stories—past, present, and perhaps even future. All I knew was that Muzzie had a friend. It seemed to make her days more bearable. Mrs. Barton would always pack a box of cookies or a cake for Muzzie to bring home to us, making the lady one of our friends as well.

When she would come back from one of her "Mrs. Barton" visits, Muzzie would tell us about the woman and explain that she was a pioneering and compassionate socialite from Baltimore. At age sixteen, Mrs. Barton had been stricken with rheumatic fever and confined to her bed. During that period of convalescence, her best companions became her beloved pets. From that experience, she vowed to devote her life to the care and treatment of companion and service animals. Once the truth came out, and Mrs. Barton learned of the plight of our family—how we had been reduced to living just above the poverty line in a garage apartment and how my dad was rarely able to find work—she offered my mother what she hoped would be a solution.

Mrs. Barton had recently purchased a home five miles out of town for the purpose of establishing a local Humane Society. She offered Muzzie the chance to run the local Humane Society from the house, suggesting that instead of rent, we could take on the responsibility of being in charge of the animals. All we would have to do was take in and register the strays that came in, and then lead them to the backyard kennels. When people showed an interest in adopting one of the animals, it was our responsibility to convince that person that a forever home for the dog was the right thing to do. The house was small, Mrs. Barton explained, but we would be able to move in any time that suited us. It had hot water, heat, and newly upgraded electricity. Raising her eyes to the heavens, Muzzie's faith was reaffirmed.

While we jumped for joy to be leaving the garage apartment, the fact that we were leaving the beach also made us sad. Muzzie rationalized that at least we'd have a home, a yard, and besides, fall was just around the corner, putting an end to beach weather.

For the next four years, the five of us, plus Coolie when he was around, lived in the little house called the Humane Society. It had one bedroom downstairs, a small living room, a proper kitchen, and an upstairs attic. We kids slept in the attic. There were even a couple of rocking chairs out on the front porch, and a tire swing hanging from one of the front yard trees. It was a joyful day when we lugged our four mattresses out from the floor of the garage apartment. Less so when we discovered that we had to lug all of them up the ladder staircase to our attic loft. It was a sad day, though, when winter came. We quickly realized that the one heater for the entire house was on the main floor, and it simply was not powerful enough to push the heat and funnel the warmth upstairs to the attic. Whatever warm air that did come into the attic came through a small grate in the floor. Many was the night that I crawled off my mattress and laid on top of that grate, just to warm my frozen bones, annoying my siblings as they tried to sleep in that attic's cold.

The thought of that cold attic room still gives me chills when I think of it now.

3
My Reality Check

It was August 1961, and on Sundays it was always "Dinner at Muzzie's." All of us children were then grown, and we had all chipped in to help my brother, Lynn, build a three-story apartment building in Ocean City, which included two separate apartments and a total of five bedrooms. The idea was to provide my parents with both a place to live, as well as a steady source of income. When the building had been completed, my mother quickly took charge and rented out all the rooms to the summertime workers. Muzzie and Coolie had gone through a lot over the years, including eleven moves. Now, however, they finally had some stability in their lives. In spite of all the difficulties we had gone through as a family, the one thing that we all looked forward to was the Sundays that we would spend together.

As children, no matter where we lived, Sunday dinners were special. Muzzie would make pot roast, chili con carne, or corned beef and cabbage as the meal of the day. For us kids, Sunday's dishes were always the meal of the week. Muzzie wasn't the most brilliant cook, but her Irish roots would kick in and she would get inspired—mainly when supplies were limited, and our tummies were rumbling. When we were poor, it no doubt took creativity for her to feed five kids when all my mother usually had in her pocket were mere nickels and dimes. She had developed a true talent for turning a pound of hamburger meat into a simple but delicious cottage pie that put smiles on all our young faces.

My wife, Mike, and I lived about thirty miles from my parents' new place, and we always looked forward to Muzzie's Sunday dinners. Being married, with two kids and a third on the way, left little money in our own coffers for a good dinner, so her invitations were always appreciated. We would make the weekly journey with expectant smiles on our faces, counting every mile of the way. Little did I know, however, that by the end of this particular Sunday dinner, Muzzie would throw me a stomach punch that set my life in an entirely new direction. A life that would never be the same as it was that day before we left our twelve-foot wide trailer in a suburb of Salisbury, Maryland called Fruitland.

That morning, Muzzie had called and I picked up the phone. "I'm preparing Sunday dinner. You are coming, right?" Muzzie asked in a voice that made it sound more like a command than an invitation. "You, Mike, and the kids—I want you here a little earlier than usual."

"You can count on it," I replied. There was something in her voice, though, that faintly triggered a hazard signal in my head. I knew Muzzie's moods, having been on the receiving end of them since I was a child. So as I hung up the telephone, a part of me knew that a mess of dark clouds were gathering on the horizon of this unseasonably cold summer Sunday.

The drive to Muzzie's normally took us about a half-hour. Silence pervaded the air during this particular ride. Mike was alerted to my silence and asked, "Are you okay? I've been talking to you and you haven't said a word back. You've been awfully quiet."

Her voice shook me out of my trip back in time. "Huh?" I said. "No, I'm okay. Um, just keeping my eyes open, looking for a gas station. What were you saying?" Mike knew not to press. Whatever was bothering me would come out in the end, as it always did. But what she didn't know was that Muzzie was riding along there in the front seat with us.

The children loved going to Muzzie's house for Sunday dinner, so it was their squealing and clapping as we turned down the street leading to her house that quickly brought an end to my memories of being a child living in Ocean City. A few minutes later we were pulling into Muzzie's driveway, where her greeting shook me right back into the present. "Go wash your hands and get the kids ready for dinner." That's all she said. No hug. No smile. Mike looked at me, shrugged, and walked into the house. It was obvious something was up. I just didn't know what, and I wasn't planning to ask. Mike and the kids were looking forward to the meal, and that was enough for me.

The dinner table conversation was forced. Tension filled the air. Muzzie sat there, crossing and uncrossing her arms, glancing at me uneasily. We finished the meal in silence.

After dinner, Mike took the kids outside to play, leaving me alone with my mother. She and I silently cleared the table, passing each other as we went back and forth from the kitchen but never touching. My heart kept racing with every dirty dish that I put into the sink, and I found myself wishing that I could disappear. I knew in my gut that whatever was ahead of us that evening was sure to be a humdinger.

Muzzie had always been a no-nonsense person. She would sometimes say things to other family members that would make one or the other of them visibly quiver in fear and intimidation. I couldn't begin to guess what she was about to say to me. I knew one thing, though: I had remained her favorite, when it came to her children. She had no qualms about displaying this preference of hers to others either. I kept reminding myself of that, hoping it would help subdue my anxiety. It almost worked, right up until the moment when she sat me down at the dinner table and began to speak.

"Let me get straight to the point," she said in a tightly controlled tone. "It's time you accept responsibility. Not just for yourself, but for those beautiful children of yours. Look at where you are today. You're twenty-six years old. Left and right, you throw away opportunities that come your way. Who does that?"

I started to say something in my defense, but Muzzie shut me up. When she got on a roll, as I was now being reminded of all over again, there was nothing that could stop her.

"Your part-time teaching job barely covers the rent and puts food on the table, and you're living in a damn trailer park! When the hell are you going to grow up? When are you going to stop running away from responsibility? Or are you satisfied being a failure, with no future planned whatsoever?"

There was nothing that I could say. The fear that I had anticipated was justified. I had no defense against anything she was saying. And she still wasn't finished, as what had been only minutes seemed to pass like hours for me. It was as if she unrolled my life up until then and had carefully compiled a list of everything in which I had been a total failure.

"You threw away a college scholarship. The Army didn't make a man out of you. And you squandered two years at the university in College Park before dropping out—just so you could spend the summer drinking beer and getting married. For heaven's sake, what were you thinking? Life isn't a joke! You think that getting married and having kid after kid makes you a man? Take off your blinders, before your wife and kids realize just who and what you are and pack their bags. It's your choice, son."

I sat stunned, as she walked out of the room. No one had ever verbally beat me down before as she had just then. Looking back all these years later, I realize how hard it must have been for her to lay me out like that. But she did, and I was dazed. It took me a while to gather myself together—then I walked to the open front door and told Mike to get our things. We were leaving. I tried to hug Muzzie, but her staunch posture told me that my hands on her arms was as close as I was going to get. As I walked through the open door, I turned around and said, "I'm sorry, Mom. I know you love me, but I need some time to figure this out on my own."

The ride back to our trailer park was the longest ride of my life. I flicked on the car radio. Mike turned it off. The air was so heavy with tension that even the kids in the back seat sensed it, and they remained uncharacteristically quiet.

"Are you going to talk about it?" Mike asked. "Or are you going to brood at the wheel all the way home?"

"It was awful," I stammered. "She told me in no uncertain terms that I needed to get my shit together. She said that I was a goddamn failure. How's that for a happy Sunday dinner?"

"Watch your language in front of the kids!" Mike shushed. But after a moment, one that was heavy with the history of the two of us and the emotions we had shared, she asked, "Well, do you think your mother was right? Do *you* believe you're a failure? That's what's important here."

We were at a red light, and I sat as the light turned green, then red again. Mike just stared at me, the pregnant wife with a pregnant question. Fidgeting behind the wheel, I pondered Mike's question. Muzzie had opened a Pandora's box, and Mike was now helping to nudge me into that box.

Finally, I heard myself confess in a voice barely above a whisper. "We can't keep living like this." The rest of the drive home was heavy with silence.

It's not easy finding a quiet place to think when you live in a twelve-foot wide trailer and have two rowdy kids competing for attention. I tried, but even the tiny bathroom wasn't insulated from the noise. Mike was at the table next to our galley-style kitchen, head in hands when I walked past her, picked up the car keys, and said, "I'm going out for a while." She looked up and into my eyes, knowing I needed some space to think and said simply, "Come back when you have answers."

I said, "Whether I have the answers or not, you know I'm coming back. I just have to be alone."

Standing in the driveway, I looked around at our shabby existence. Even in our lowest times growing up, we never equated ourselves with trailer-park life. For us, it was the lowest of the low. When the wind was blowing in our direction, the stench of the chicken farms surrounding our town made us run for cover. My car was held together with duct tape, and black smoke accompanied us wherever we drove. How had I let this happen? How could I have done this to the woman I loved? To my kids? Just a few years back, I had been the happiest man alive when she said she'd marry me. I'd been living in a bubble, coasting, and until Muzzie threw my life in my face, I never considered my future.

Backing out of the driveway, I had no idea where I was going. I just needed quiet. A place to think. I remembered as a kid that I would walk the Ocean City Boardwalk, the sweet salt air replacing any fuzz that had gathered and was swimming in my brain. That's where I'd go. The beach. Maybe it would still have its magic.

I found a spot on a bluff overlooking the Atlantic Ocean and parked, rolled down the windows, and inhaled deeply. My head rested back on the seat, my eyes closed. I could feel the tears welling up under my eyelids. Muzzie's words echoed in my head. *When are you going to grow up, Fred? Or are you satisfied being a failure?* A failure? Was I? I needed a sign. Some direction. Anything that would take me from my life of acceptance to one that gave me the drive to go further. What would it take to make Mike proud of me? Make me proud of myself? I knew I had Muzzie's love, but what I had lost was her respect, and I needed to win it back.

Nothing. No lightning bolt. No incredible plan. Answers weren't coming to me, just questions. Why did I throw away that wrestling scholarship to West Virginia that was offered to me when I graduated high school? To play on the beach and party? Why did I walk out on my second chance for a college degree when I left the Army and went to the university in College Park? Again, a wrestling scholarship was waved in my face. Sure, I wasn't thrilled about the sport of wrestling, but why couldn't I have used it to get an education? To make a career for myself? What was wrong with me? Now looking back, it seemed so obvious. My future was handed to me on a platter and I tossed it away to become what? A failure.

So much for the salt air clearing my brain. I sat there, feeling the hollowness of what lay ahead. I needed to shake the comforts of my irresponsible past out of my existence and replace them with the responsible husband, father and son I knew I could be, but had never tried to be. Muzzie's chiding voice kept ringing in my ears. Many times I'd heard her say in the past, *Necessity is the mother of invention.* I needed to invent.

When I got home, it was late, and everyone was sleeping. I quietly crawled into my side of the bed, so as not to wake Mike, but I tossed and turned so much that night that it's a wonder the sheets weren't full of holes the next morning. Foreboding thoughts rolled around in my head, feeling like a steel ball bouncing around in an arcade machine. What should I do? Where do I begin? I can't go on living without a future plan. I knew I would only be happy if the answer had something to do with sports. A physical education teacher? A coach? What I did know was that every time I envisioned my life in the future, it was filled with a passion for a career in sports.

I still had my part-time job at the local Catholic school but dreaded going there. Sister Angela pleaded with me to tackle math with her middle-schoolers. I couldn't say no. We needed the extra income, so I reluctantly agreed. Oh, how I hated it. My unorthodox method of teaching mathematical reasoning ended up with one kid breaking a window. Shattered glass was splayed everywhere. The job provided us just enough money to squeak by, and the occasional jobs I had playing in my brother Lynn's band kept the creditors away. I was like a lost animal in the wild looking for comfort, and just getting by was no longer an option. I needed something that would make me happy in the future. No way was I going to stay where I was, dreading teaching subjects the kids probably knew more about than I did. And Muzzie's browbeating was a constant reminder of my failure.

A few months before, I had received a call from an acquaintance who asked if I would be interested in selling insurance. The job would provide me the security I needed for our family. It would show those who doubted me that I now had a steady decent paying job. Mike and I discussed it. She knew in my heart that I wouldn't be happy as an insurance salesman. Coolie's failure was bound to become my failure, and I wasn't traveling down that road. She said, "You'll have to find out what the answer is for you, but I know it isn't insurance."

Oh, how lucky to have a wife who has trust and confidence in me, or did she still? I questioned. I put my head back down onto the pillow and must have drifted back to when I was a kid, shooting hoops in the backyard of the Humane Society house. My makeshift basketball court became my arena. I wouldn't stop dribbling and shooting until I'd made twenty-one points without missing a basket. With the roar of cheering fans echoing in my head, I'd play until all the lights in the house came on and the smell of dinner pierced the air. *I want to be back in that arena*, were the words that hit me as my eyes opened for the second time.

At about nine in the morning, I rolled over, knowing that this Monday was an "off" day for Catholic schools in the area. I reached over and turned on the radio to listen to a popular talk show and heard the announcer say, "Today, we're talking to Coach 'Pop' Watson, the head of the Physical Education department from Maryland State College in Princess Anne.

I listened, drifting in and out of consciousness as the show's host continued to talk to the coach. But when Coach Watson started talking about the sports programs offered at Maryland State, I sat up. The announcer had asked, "So, other than the winning football team you have there at Maryland State, what other programs have you put on the schedule?"

"Well, we've expanded our already great Physical Education department. The board decided to add a four-year Bachelor of Science or Bachelor of Science Education degree," the coach said.

With that, I turned the volume up. I sat up in bed and zoned into what the coach was saying. "Teaching credentials are important to our student body. A full-blown Physical Education curriculum, complete with a four-year teaching degree, would put them in a prime position to be hired by any school anywhere in the state."

Wait! What did he just say? A degree in Physical Education? Hell, this could be what I've been looking for. Damn!

Muzzie had nailed it on the head. I had wasted two years at the University of Maryland's College Park campus and squandered my wrestling scholarship so I could party in Ocean City. This guy on the radio was telling me that that could all change. I could carve a new path. Before this moment, I didn't have a vision for my future—I had no passion, nothing exciting to look forward to. Just last evening, I had felt hopeless. Now, this guy, whether he knew it or not, laid out an opportunity for someone he didn't know—me. And it could be Maryland State College. Wherever that was.

"Mike," I yelled, jumping from the bed and practically falling into the living area. "Isn't Maryland State College somewhere near here?"

"Yeah. In Princess Anne," she answered, barely looking up from the sink full of dirty breakfast dishes. "Why?"

"Because you're not going to believe what I just heard on the radio," I said, holding my hands up high above my head in a "V for Victory" salute. "They're introducing a four-year Physical Education major in the fall semester. I could enroll and finish my degree there and could become a real teacher, not the half-assed pretend teacher that I've been for all these years."

Mike slowly put down the dish sponge, wiped her hands, picked up her cup of coffee that had gone cold by now, turned around, and just looked at me as if I were nuts. "You're the wrong color, mister—Maryland State is an all-Black school. You didn't know that?"

Her words hung in the air for what seemed like an eternity.

"Shit! You're kidding me?" And now my words hung in the air. "Hold it, you mean only Black kids go to Maryland State?"

"I think that's been the case since it was opened. I don't know if it's changed since then. And if it hasn't, what makes you think that a white man is going to be able to just waltz in, register, and be accepted?"

"But the College Park campus has Black and white students. Why wouldn't Maryland State? They're both state schools," I asked, getting more and more frustrated as the answer to my newly found plan was slowly being taken away from me.

"You're getting delirious," Mike yelled angrily. "Where does it say that a white man is going to be accepted into a Black school? Have you listened to the news lately? There's a Black man who keeps trying to get into the all-white University of Mississippi. You know what'll happen when he pushes the issue. The Supreme Court be damned! That Jim Crow state won't stand for it. People will die. What makes you think the same thing won't happen here if you try to register at that Black college?"

Mike was the sensible one. What she was saying rang true.

"You realize that this might be my, or should I say 'our' last chance?" I said, in a pleading voice. "We don't know what's going on at that school. Mississippi isn't Maryland, and this idea, this chance has dropped into our laps. At least give me your okay to check it out. To see if it's an option."

Mike and I had quarreled before, like most married couples. But this time was different. She was digging her heels in, and her fear was for me—for *us*.

"I'm afraid for you. For us. Maybe we should go back to College Park where you started. We can ask my dad for the money to move the trailer," she said.

"To where? A better trailer park! No! No more hand-outs," I said. "He's given us enough. It's time for me to step up to the plate."

"And if you find yourself causing demonstrations, is that fair to the kids, to me . . . if anything happens to you? Is that what you *want*?!"

"Mike, this is Eastern Shore Maryland. If there was anything going on at Maryland State, don't you think we would have heard about it?"

"How long do you think it will take them to see you as a white outsider, keeping another Black student from getting into their college?" Mike's face was filled with anger and fear, and she headed down the small hallway to our bedroom.

"Mike, don't be like that. Just give it a chance, please."

"How are we going to pay for all this? College costs money!"

Mike had hit a nerve with that question. With two kids, a baby on the way, doctor and hospital bills sitting in unopened envelopes on the dining room table, we were living on the edge. Like we always were.

I never gave a thought about the important parts of being a husband and father. I knew I drove her crazy whenever I said, "We'll get by," as she waved another bill in front of my face.

"I'll get Sister Angela to adjust my schedule once I get my courses laid out. I can still play in my brother's band at night and on weekends for extra money . . . and besides, I'd be an in-state student with very little tuition to pay. The only other things I'd have to worry about are books, but maybe that'll be covered by the G.I. bill. I'll have to check it out."

The look of desperation on my face must have melted her resolve because she softened. All too often in our marriage, she knew that I preferred doing things the easy way—and she always stood by my side in those instances. She had never put me down or embarrassed me. That apparently was going to be Muzzie's job. But for the first time, I was taking the hard road and while I knew Mike loved me, I needed to commit to something, not just because of what Muzzie said, but because it was time.

"Mike," I said, with every shred of dignity that I could muster, "if I don't do this, then I *am* going nowhere. Is that what you want for me?"

Mike shot back at me quickly with, "Don't put this back on me! You've had years to figure out where you were going! Now, all of a sudden, someone on the radio gives you an idea, and here you are—running out the door and signing up to go to an all-Black college? No matter the consequences to yourself—not to mention me and the kids?"

"Mike, just let me check it out. If it turns out to be dangerous, or uncomfortable, or if I'm not accepted, I'll just turn around and forget about it. We'll find another way. But I need to try. Please, just go along with me—and if I hit a brick wall, I won't mention it again."

"I might as well be talking to that brick wall over there," Mike said with frustration. "I'll make a deal with you. You go there and try to register. If there is one bit of danger, or anger coming from their students that is aimed at you, then you have to agree that your idea goes out the window. Deal?"

"Deal," I muttered, following Mike back into the kitchen and picking up the dish towel to dry all the breakfast dishes. I turned to look at her but didn't see the smile I expected. Just a look of concern. *Give it time,* I thought to myself. Besides, what other choice did I have?

I spent the next few weeks researching the school at our local library and read the catalogs that they sent with a growing sense of excitement. I checked out my G.I. Bill eligibility and found it still applied to my education. I got a copy of my transcripts from the College Park campus to see what credits could then be transferred and established my in-state residency for the reduced-fee tuition. Open enrollment for Maryland residents was a godsend. I was determined. I had a goal. And for the first time in a very long time, I was excited watching the pile of information grow larger every day. My future was in that pile.

I laid in bed the night before registration, excited about what lay ahead, yet my stomach was churning thinking about what it'd be like when I crossed the line into an all-African American culture. Even when I was in the Army and segregation was coming to an end in the Armed Forces, there was still an undercurrent of separation between Black and white enlistees. This was going to be a totally new experience for me, and one that I would have to face with as much determination as I could muster. I had never given it much thought when I would see a Black person in a crowd of all-white people. I never wondered what it would be like in reverse.

I was about to find out.

1961 TIMELINE

January 6, 1961. Federal Judge William A. Bootle ordered that the University of Georgia allow admission to the school's first two Black students, Charlayne Hunter and Hamilton Holmes. The state's appeal to the Supreme Court was denied and Hunter and Holmes arrived on campus to jeers from white students. Following a riotous mob attack on Hunter's dormitory, U of GA suspended Holmes and Hunter for their own safety.

February 12, 1961. The "Jail-No-Bail" tactic was taken to York County Prison Farm located in Rock Hill, South Carolina, where SNCC leaders and over 300 protesters picketed for the release of ten students imprisoned for sitting in at the McCrory lunch counter, and setting the stage for the Freedom Riders choosing jail over bail.

May 4, 1961. The Freedom Riders launched their protest by departing Washington, D.C. on a Greyhound bus, led by CORE Director James Farmer. Thirteen Freedom Riders (7 Black, 6 white), including John Lewis, planned to reach New Orleans by May 17th where they would pay tribute to the Supreme Court decision, Brown v. Board of Education, ruling that segregation in public schools was unconstitutional. Thrown out of the local Greyhound waiting rooms and directed toward the areas reserved for "colored," violence intensified. Lewis was beaten and left on a sidewalk. No arrests were made.

May 20, 1961. Fearing a KKK ambush, the State of Alabama sends police protection to the Freedom Riders as they traveled from Birmingham to Montgomery. Police disappeared before the bus reached the terminal and riders were greeted by hundreds of Klansmen and intense rioting ensued. Several riders were hospitalized.

September 20, 1961. James Meredith, backed by the 1954 Brown v. Board of Education Supreme Court ruling that segregation in schools was illegal, tried to register as a student at the University of Mississippi. He was unsuccessful and was personally blocked by Governor Ross Barnett.

September 25, 1961. Herbert Lee murdered. The Black father of nine, a founding member of the NAACP in Amite County, Mississippi, and voter registration advocate was shot in the head by State Assemblyman E. H. Hurst as he tried to deliver cotton to the local gin. More than ten witnesses refused to implicate the 6'3" Hurst who pleaded "self-defense" against the 5'4" Lee. Hurst never spent a day in jail.

November 8, 1961. CORE's Route 40 Protest began when Blacks were being denied service in roadside stops along the Baltimore to Wilmington, Delaware corridor Federal Highway. On this date, CORE declared a partial victory with half of the 47 restaurants relenting. President Kennedy stepped in and called for voluntary cooperation for an immediate end to segregation in restaurants and other places of public service on U.S. 40 in Maryland.

December 1961. Martin Luther King and the SCLC joined the Albany Movement, a desegregation coalition. After a mass arrest of peaceful demonstrators King declined bail until the city made desegregation concessions.

4

Maryland State College

While I now knew that Maryland State College offered a Bachelor's Degree in Physical Education and it was a historically all-Black college, I knew very little about the school itself. I read up on it in the Salisbury library, where I learned a great deal more about its history.

Since its founding in 1886 as a religious-backed academy, the school had gone through several name changes and transformations. For much of its early history, it had provided an agricultural-based education. It was renamed Maryland State Agricultural College for Negroes in 1894. Always fighting to retain its state funding, looking for qualified teachers and always pushing to grow its academic offerings, the school struggled with the state legislators and their intent to keep Black students separated from whites. It was not until 1954, when the Supreme Court passed legislation outlawing segregation in schools, that a handful of Black students were accepted into the other branches of the Maryland State college system. But the school I was about to head off to had been serving Maryland's Black community for nearly one hundred years, and had stayed segregated. It hadn't yet enrolled its first white person. As I headed toward the Princess Anne campus my hope was that they would allow me, a white person, to earn the degree I should have had by now.

The school was about twenty-five miles from my home. Having plotted my drive, I figured it would take me a half-hour to get there. Registration would begin at nine o'clock and I wanted to leave a good hour to drive, find out where I was going, and get a feel for the place. Trying to be calm, I kissed Mike good-bye, grabbed the envelope from the table containing my application forms and transcripts, and walked out of our trailer and toward the beginning of what I hoped was going to be the answer to my prayers—and Muzzie's.

When I was growing up, my family never talked about Black people and our different cultures. It never faced racism straight-on. We knew African-American people lived on their side of town, and we lived on ours. But we never used the derogatory terms about Black people that were all too commonly heard everywhere. I lived in a white culture and here I was, heading toward a school where the African-American culture dominated. It was different, I had to admit, but I wasn't going to let nerves stop me from what I was about to do.

Eighteen miles to go, I said to myself as I pulled onto Route 13, the road leading to Maryland State College. *Thank you, Muzzie, for kicking me in the ass. I needed that! And thank you, Mike, for . . . for being Mike.*

The exit sign for Princess Anne couldn't come soon enough. Traveling down the highway, contemplating my arrival at Maryland State College, my mind filled with thoughts of how the world I lived in still segregated the races. The Civil War had freed the slaves, and parts of Maryland had fought on the side of the North, but the Eastern Shore sided with the South. The lines that existed today were as clear as the sign on public bathrooms stating "Whites Only." I knew what was going on, but really, there was very little I could do. Whether I thought it was fair or not had nothing to do with what had existed around me all my life.

The fact was that while I may have been raised in a family who were kind and thoughtful, it didn't mean Black people were welcomed into our home as guests. When my mother opened her boarding house in Ocean City, she would tell every Black person looking to rent a room to come to the back door. She feared someone would see her talking to a Black person. And, of course, when they reached the back door, she would tell them that she had no rooms. When you are instilled with the divisions of a white-black society, it lives in you in strange ways. My mother may have been subtle about it, but she was a racist. She never talked mean about Black people, and we weren't raised to speak that way either. And while I don't think I ever judged a person by the color of his skin, I just accepted these racial divides as normal.

Funny how the mind works. It seemed seconds since I had pulled out of our trailer's parking spot. But there the sign was, in front of me . . . *PRINCESS ANNE NEXT RIGHT*. A burning lump tightened in my throat. The moment was here. All the procrastinating, wavering, and hesitation was over. I exited the road and turned toward the campus, and staring at me was what could be the game-changer of my life. *WELCOME TO MARYLAND STATE COLLEGE.*

From that moment on, my whole outlook changed. All the negative thoughts that had run through my mind, all the hesitation Mike and I had discussed, slowly dissipated. I was stoked. With a sense of calm and ease, I drove through the entrance to the campus of Maryland State College. In an instant, the world I had known since birth changed from white to black. There before me, milling about were young Black people with not a white face anywhere. I wavered for a few minutes. This is not a joke. This is reality. I wasn't on my turf, this was theirs. I bolstered my courage by remembering I hadn't turned back when I had to go out on the mat for the finals of National Prep School Wrestling Championships years before. I was nervous then, as I was now. But I didn't walk away. I didn't give in.

Peering over the well-manicured landscape, I looked for a sign directing me to REGISTRATION. Two young Black guys who seemed to be students walked toward my car. I sucked it in, rolled down my window, and asked if they could tell me where the Registration building was.

One of them asked, "Why? You looking for a job?"

"No," I said, "I'm looking to enroll."

"Man, you realize this school is for Black folk, don't you?" he said sarcastically, as I stopped beside them.

"I do," I said.

They stared at me for several moments, the air thick with words that weren't being said. "You trying to be one of those protesters for the rights of white people, huh?" the other said with a sly grin on his face. "I hear the white people in Mississippi are talking about hanging any Black person who comes onto their sacred campus. You think people around here might do the same to you if you try to register?"

I thought back to my agreement with Mike that morning. If I felt threatened, my plan would be over.

"It's not gonna happen," I said, staring the kid in the eye and speaking in a soft voice. "I'm not here to make trouble. I'm here to get an education and my degree, same as you." Surprised by my conviction, the other kid said, "Man, you gotta be crazy but, whatever—turn up that road to the left. You'll see a dark brick building covered with ivy. That's where you register. Good luck!" he said, shaking his head in disbelief. "Maybe I'll see you in class!"

About three hundred yards in the distance sat a two-story red-brick building. It looked like it had been built around the turn of the century. The windows were barely visible from the heavy ivy vines tugging at its exterior. As I got closer, I could see through the open pane windows that people were in line, chatting and waiting. Surely, this was the right place. I found a parking lot and threw my car into the closest spot available. I was in a hurry to get things done, but first I had to summon up my other-self.

Back when I was in the Army, a fellow soldier gave me a piece of advice that never left me. We'd just finished eight weeks of grueling training. Each of us was being called into the Sergeant's office to discuss the outcome of that training and where we were to go from there. I broke out in a sweat as my name inched closer to the top of the list, and it was Hooty McCoy who told me to walk into the room with a smile on my face. "Act it, and you will become it," he said. "Show him a man filled with confidence. A man who knows where he's going in life. You might be shitting in your pants, but don't let Sarge know it. Or smell it!"

Students were gathered on the steps of the building, checking out each other's class schedules and talking like any group of college kids would. Almost in unison, they looked with uncertainty at me as I walked through them on my way to the entrance.

I opened the door quickly, stepped inside, and came face-to-face with about fifty other people—students waiting to register and a group of adults handling the paperwork. The students turned to look at me. The adults looked up from their tables to look at me as well. I stood there, feeling stark naked. My body felt as if it was closing in on itself while they looked me over as if I were a strange animal that had crawled out of an open place on the wall. They turned around in unison, their mouths agape, their expressions saying, "What the hell are you doing here?" I may have wanted to walk out of the building, jump in the car, and speed home, but I wasn't going to let that happen.

Finally, I sucked up enough courage to say, "Good morning," in my most confident of voices to the person in front of me. She was an attractive young Black girl, and looked almost as nervous as me. *Act it, and you will become it,* rang in my head.

She politely turned and said, "If you're looking for the delivery entrance, I think it's in the building next door."

"Actually, I'm looking to enroll for the fall semester," I said in a voice loud enough for the rest of those in line to hear. I could hear a few hushed comments being made around me, but it was not going to stop me from doing what I needed to do.

It seemed like an eternity, waiting in line. The knots in my stomach tightened in anticipation. Finally, the middle-aged Black lady sitting at the table in front of me looked up and said, "Next."

I stepped up to the table.

"This line is for students," she said.

I said, "I am a student . . . I mean, I *want* to be a student. I'm here to enroll in classes."

"You know this is a school for Black students?"

"I'm here to get a degree in Physical Education. Don't you accept white students?"

She gave me a puzzled look and said, "Wait here. I need to talk to the Registrar."

She went into an office directly behind her. A few minutes later, a Black man opened the door to his office, peered out at me, and then ducked back inside. A few minutes after that, the lady emerged from the office and sat back down in her seat.

"Well, it turns out, you have the right to enroll in this school," she stated, "but it just so happens that you'd be the first white person ever to do so." With that, she then said, "Can I see your admission form and your transcript, please?"

I confidently opened the envelope I had brought with me, only to pull out papers filled with colorful drawings done by my children—as I could see their names proudly scrawled on the bottom of each work of art.

I'm pretty sure the advice Hooty gave me didn't cover this from happening at my sergeant interview, but I needed to take a breath and say something . . . anything!

"Ahhhh" was about the only thing that came out of my mouth, but I needed more. "I . . . I'm sorry. I must have grabbed the wrong envelope when I left the house this morning."

The woman laughed. I laughed. And as she carefully looked at each picture, she said, "My kids did the same thing. Only they didn't expect them to be used as college transcripts! I hope you're not using these to get into the Art curriculum!" She then tucked them back into the envelope and said, "We're here tomorrow. Come back with the right envelope, and we'll see if we can get you started on that degree."

I looked around embarrassingly to see the faces of others. One guy was coughing like a drink had gone down the wrong way. Another was reassuring others that what they had just heard was gospel truth. A few looked at me with pity.

I asked her, "What time do you close? If I come back later with the information you need, can I register for classes?"

"We close at nine tonight. We're here late because a lot of our students work during the day."

"Thank you. I'll be back either later today or tomorrow." And with that, I turned to walk through the maze of onlookers to find my way out the door. As I reached the exit, there stood a Black guy who was so huge he would have made two of me. Walking past this behemoth of a man, I heard him say, "What's up? Won't they let you register?"

Damn, that's the scariest person I've ever seen, I thought to myself, too embarrassed to respond. I just kept walking across the lawn and towards my car. But my car wasn't there. I looked in all directions, but no car. A police car came slowly rolling by with a Black officer behind the wheel, and I raised my hand to try to get his attention, but he continued on. He then turned around and came back to where I was standing.

I'm sure he wondered what I was doing out in front of the Registration building and would question why I was there. When he pulled up, I politely told him that I was attempting to register for school but didn't have the proper papers. He asked if I had my driver's license. I did, and he scanned it with his eyes, devouring every letter and number. "So, you want to register here?" he asked. "This is Maryland State College. You sure you got the right place?"

"Yes, sir," I replied. He looked again at my license, turning it up and down, back and forth in his hands.

He then took things to a different level when he asked if I was a government agent. He was convinced that something was strange about me wanting to go to an all-Black college. While he kept pressing me, he suggested that perhaps I was trying to infiltrate the campus. Maybe I would try to cause some disturbance. Then the Black students would get the blame.

"Sir, I just want to find my car and go home. That's all."

Little did I know that all this time the big guy from the Registration building was still across the lawn, witnessing all of what was happening to me. He slowly walked toward us. The cop eyed him. As he approached, the big guy said, "George, is this white guy bothering you?" And he laughed.

George was obviously the cop's name, and George asked him, "You know him?"

The big guy said, "Yeah. He's going to be a student." From there, things changed in a heartbeat when the big guy told the policeman that I just needed a little help.

It didn't take thirty seconds before the officer told me that the car was in the impound lot for parking illegally. That was the good news. The bad news was that it would cost me five dollars to get it back. I had some cash in my pocket. I told the officer that's all I had. The cop turned to the big guy and said, "Should I let him go?" The big guy asked him to give me a break. That I'd probably missed the No Parking sign hidden behind the trees. The officer then said jokingly, "Works for me. Just keep doing what you do on the football field this season, and we'll all be happy!" The officer offered to drive me to the lot and as I got into his car, I nodded thanks to the big guy while digging into my pocket for my five dollars. The cop said I could keep my money, and that if I was a friend of Bob's, I was a friend of his.

I wasn't a friend of Bob's before that day, but I vowed to make him my friend. He went to bat for me and didn't even know me. Maybe Mike had a lot less to worry about than she knew.

I sped home that afternoon, anxious to tell Mike of the day's experience. As I pulled down the lane to our trailer, there was Mike standing at the door, fingering the necklace I had bought her for

Mother's Day with one hand and pulling the envelope containing my registration papers from behind her back. She was shaking her head as she approached the driver's side of the car, and as I opened it, we both broke out in laughter.

I told her about the lady at the Registration table and how she laughed, looking at the childish drawings, and inferred I would never be an Art major! As we walked to the trailer, I told her that our worries were unfounded. With the exception of a few incredulous stares, there were no resentments toward my being there. I purposely left out my confrontation with the parking police.

The next day, I drove to the school with all my papers in hand. I'd checked and double-checked that I had the right envelope and went with confidence, hoping the same lady would be at the Registration desk. I found a legal spot to park, went straight to the Registration building, found the lady I'd spoken to the day before, and by the time I left, I was registered as a Physical Education major for the coming semester's classes. It all went off without a hitch.

Sunday's dinner at Muzzie's couldn't come soon enough. I'd spoken with my brother Lynn the night before, telling him what I had planned to do, and where. But the big test was Muzzie. I just wasn't sure how she would take it.

Driving toward Ocean City, a little voice from the back seat said, "Daddy, are you going back to school with Black kids?"

I sucked in my breath for a moment and started telling them a story from my childhood. If anything, it would keep them quiet for the rest of the trip.

"Let me tell you about when I was your age and we lived in what was called the Humane Society house in Ocean City. Grandma Muzzie had her eggs delivered by a Black lady named Thelma Cropper.

"Every Saturday morning Thelma would drive her egg route, delivering eggs up and down the countryside. She would climb out of her old truck, holding the basket of eggs for my mother, look over and yell, 'Hello, Freddy.' I held my breath most times, hoping she wouldn't drop any eggs.

"One morning, as I looked down the road, there was Thelma and her old Chevy making its way to our house. I often wondered how that truck ever made its rounds. The front end would wobble and clank. The tires were probably the same ones from the day she bought the thing from Ed Fears, who lived across the street from us. And the back window was taped with some kind of glue over newspapers.

"When Thelma got closer to our driveway, I spotted someone else in the truck. It looked like a young Black boy about my age. Sure enough, it was."

"'Hello, Freddy,' Thelma yelled out the window. 'Brought my son Josh with me today. Before long, he's gonna be old enough to do the route himself. Might as well get him started now.'

"Josh grabbed the basket with our eggs. Together, he and Thelma walked toward the front porch where they'd wait for Muzzie to come out. When they were about halfway there, I said to Josh, 'Hey, you want to see where we keep the dogs?'

"'Sure,' he said, turning his eyes toward his mother for her approval.

"Josh was tall and wore baggy pants where the knees on both legs were worn through. He seemed nervous walking with me. Black kids never were seen hanging around white kids. I didn't care. I just yearned to have someone other than my older brother and sisters to talk to.

"All eight of the dog kennels were in the back of our house, cages with tightly woven chicken wire surrounding each kennel. This day there were eight dogs in each kennel, and they barked as Josh and I walked by. I felt for the dogs. Their whining barks conjured up the thought that they hoped that someone would come by to adopt them."

"We played with the dogs for a while and started walking toward the front when two white boys from the neighborhood saw us and started marching across the lawn towards us."

"'What you doin' with this Black boy? You a n - - - - r lover?' the bigger one growled at me as he lobbed a small rock toward Josh.

"Josh stood behind me, afraid. I was, too, and stuttered, 'He's my friend.'

"'You want trouble?' the smaller boy said as he got close, his fist wrapped around another rock.

"The house was too far away to run to, and the boys stood in our way. We were trapped until Muzzie and Thelma came running around to the back, having heard the commotion. Muzzie unleashed her inner warrior woman and marched toward the two boys, the basket of eggs in her hand.

"'Get off of my property!' she yelled, and then grabbed an egg and threw it, hitting the head of the big kid. Another smashed into the smaller kid's arm. Muzzie kept tossing eggs at the boys who were screaming and oozing with egg running down their faces, before they hightailed it out of the yard, but not without landing their final volley: "N - - - - r lovers. All of you! And this isn't the end of it.'

"Thelma grabbed Josh by the neck of his shirt and, with her face inches from his, demanded to know what he did to those boys.

"'Nothin', Ma. They came at us.'

"'Is that true, Freddy? You did nothin' to them?'

"'Yes, ma'am,' I replied.

"At that point, Muzzie stepped in and said, 'Our boys are good boys. It's those damned rednecks who cause trouble.' She then looked into her basket of eggs, thought for a moment, and then, with a smile on her Princess Warrior face, asked Thelma for another few eggs! And that was the last time I saw Josh."

Giggles were heard coming from the back seat, with my oldest chanting "Muzzie, the Princess Warrior," before Mike could caution them about using the language I'd just used in my story. "We don't call people of another color by any other name than their God-given name."

My childhood stories always helped calm my nerves and entertained the kids. It gave them some insight into my upbringing, a window on how I grew up.

What I didn't tell them was that later that day, Muzzie told me she did not want me to ever play with Thelma's boy. "Just look at the trouble you got yourself into, and it's likely I won't be around if it happens again. You could get hurt."

We arrived at Muzzie's house and by then word of my college enrollment had spread like wildfire among family members, with Lynn always unable to keep a secret. The kids rushed out of the car, heading straight to the front door calling out for Muzzie and screaming "Grandma's a Princess Warrior," as the screen door slammed shut after them. "Daddy told us the story of you throwing eggs at boys in the yard!"

As I entered the house with Mike, there stood Muzzie, with two kids wrapped into her skirts giggling and laughing, holding up what looked like a pack of matches.

"What's this?" I said, as she handed me the matchbook.

"Open it. You'll see," she said, with a grin on her face.

As I lifted up the cover, where there were once several tiers of matches with white tips, Muzzie had burned out all the white tops except one. And in the front row of all the blacked-out matches stood one lone white match. Muzzie was being funny.

It took me a few moments to get the point, and another few to figure out how I was going to handle this. I didn't want to cause a scene, not in front of Mike or the kids. And I didn't want to play into Muzzie's sarcasm, either. Tucking the matchbook into my pants pocket, I realized that this would require some delicate maneuvers on my part. The first of many I was to face in the next few years.

"Cute," was about as non-committal as I could be as the others stood there laughing, not knowing how I'd react. "What's for dinner?" I asked, quickly changing the subject.

I knew where Muzzie was coming from, but I also knew the kindness that had been shown to me when I tried to register the first time at Maryland State. I was treading between two worlds and I was heading toward one my mother would never understand.

We got home late that night. When I undressed to go to bed, I pulled the matchbook from my pocket and opened it. That packet of matches Muzzie had given me was about the only acknowledgment that I had made a decision about moving forward with my life. Neither Muzzie nor Coolie ever brought it up from that day on.

5

The Semester Begins

I woke up Monday morning feeling like a kid on his first day of school. I was excited, anxious and most of all, I was looking forward to getting on with the rest of my life. Standing in front of our little closet, crammed to the hilt with all of Mike's and my clothes, I was in a trance as I stared at the few pants and shirts in front of me.

"Mike, do you think I should wear a tie and jacket?" I asked.

"How were the other students that you saw dressed?" she replied.

"They looked like kids going to college . . . but it was Registration, so maybe they do dress up for classes."

"Okay, here's what you do. You put on a fresh pair of pants, a nice shirt, and keep a tie in your pocket, just in case. And be sure your shoes are clean. It's your first day. You'll figure it out by the last class. Sound like a plan?"

"Yes, ma'am!" I responded, as though I were back in the Army. I had my orders. I got dressed, kissed Mike and the kids good-bye, and off I went to my first day at Maryland State College.

I had to breathe in deeply as I walked to my Algebra class, a requirement that I had put off when I had gone to the College Park campus six years before. It was also a required course I had to pass in order to graduate. And it was the class I feared the most. Somehow, numbers and my brain never got along. I entered the classroom through the back door, knowing that heads would turn, and eyes would scan my face. I was definitely nervous, but I tried not to show it. I put on a smile and hoped that would be enough.

So there I was, standing in the back of the classroom, my face frozen in a pasted-on smile, not really knowing where to sit. Did my apprehension show? Thank God one of the other students, apparently noticing me standing there, unable to move and stuck to the floor, pointed me to a desk smack dab in the middle of the classroom. *Okay,* I thought to myself. *That way, the others could see me front, back, and sideways! They could also see that I was just like them. A little older, maybe, a little nervous, but no different . . . except that I was white . . . I guess that's probably how they felt when they were in a crowd of white folks. No! Focus on the front of the room, on the teacher.* While that was what I was forcing myself to think, I could still feel my heart race. I held my breath and took the desk.

Dr. Hytche was a young Black professor from Oklahoma where he'd earned his PhD from Oklahoma State University before being offered the job at Maryland State. He'd only been at Maryland State a year when he walked into the room and saw my white face sitting at a desk in the middle of a classroom filled with Black faces. He looked at me, smiled, and then welcomed all of us to his Algebra class.

Math and numbers had always been a problem for me, which is why I had put off taking this required course for as long as I could. As it turned out, Dr. Hytche had a way of teaching math that made it understandable. He taught us to read formulas like they were sentences. Our challenge was to figure out what they meant. And when one of the words were missing, usually called "X," that was the answer we needed to look for. He would explain that each solution needed a specific, step-by-step process in order to be solved. Write down the steps, cross out each step as you completed it, and you would wind up with the answer. The system that he taught the students in his class worked well for me. While that way of dealing with numbers would play out over the course of the semester, he started that first day's class with enthusiasm, encouragement, and humor. His teaching style seemed to put everyone at ease, especially me.

So many of the young professors I had in my first two years of college would teach down to their students, strutting their knowledge and reveling in all they knew and all we didn't know. Dr. Hytche wasn't like that. He had his finger on the pulse of where his students were all coming from, and made it his mission to teach in a way they would all understand. Some of my friends had chided me about going to Maryland State College, saying it was the "easy way out." That the teachers were below grade because, after all, they were educated in segregated schools by teachers who themselves went to segregated schools, and you know, the teaching in those schools was sub-par. Let me tell you, Dr. Hytche and all the other professors I had, who were all Black, were exemplary. In their hands, I felt I was well on my way, full of confidence, as the fall semester began.

In my life, there were few things that I enjoyed more than sports. I didn't just *like* sports, I *loved* sports. I had taken my core Physical Education classes at the University of Maryland, but there were some outstanding science-based classes like Psychology and Physiology of Sports that I needed to cover. I practically skipped down the walkway toward the Athletic Building and my next set of classes, all focusing on Physical Education. I had declared my major to be teaching and coaching sports because of an incident that happened when I was a youngster. It defined my life's mission.

When I was a kid, I haunted the local YMCA. Some days I would be there for more than eight hours, swimming in the pool, running on the track, or playing basketball in the gym. I'd play a basketball game by myself for hours there, shooting foul shot after foul shot. I'd run up and down that court making the imaginary game-winning shots . . . driving to the hoop and laying it in at the buzzer.

The place had a smell that I grew to love. The smell of sports, of sweat. It hovered and wafted in the air no matter where you were in the place. The clopping of feet running around the track and the clanging of weights being dropped onto mats made me feel alive. I especially liked the sound of the echo in the gym as the basketball met the wooden floor. It was a paradise—*my* paradise.

Memories of the YMCA gym flooded into my head as I entered the Athletic building and breathed in that same smell of sweat from years ago. It also brought back memories of a coach who didn't care that I was a better basketball player than his son and who failed to let me play even though our team was being slaughtered. One of my teammates tried to warn me, "You ain't gonna start . . . that's for sure. Favorites start, no matter what . . . and Coach is gonna play his son the whole game. That's a fact."

I'd bragged to my brother Rohn about how good I was, and then when he and some of his friends had come to the game to watch me play, I was never called up. As I sat on the bench the entire game, I felt such shame. I'll never forget how the coach ignored me as I sat like a keg of dynamite on the edge of the bench, waiting to get my chance. I was so worked up that I went up to the coach in the final minutes and pleaded with him, "Can I please play the last few minutes?"

Without even looking up at me, he replied, "Not this game . . . not going to happen . . . not with those dirty shoes on . . . now go sit down!"

I remember the tears forming in my eyes. I was devastated, humbled, hurt, and embarrassed. The coach not only made me feel insignificant but also humiliated me in front of the others for being poor. That hurt more than anything.

I quit the team a few weeks after that game and lost interest in practicing basketball altogether. It took almost a year before I became interested in a sport again. But it would never be a sport where I didn't have control of my game. I was (and still am) haunted by the basketball incident, scarred by that self-serving man called "Coach." The humiliation and shame of that occasion hurt, but it became my mission in life to see that those situations never happen to kids like me. Even more importantly, that coach gave me the drive to want to teach all young players that sportsmanship goes above ability. That no coach has the right to rip out the soul of a child.

Looking back, I tried to unravel why I had a "Love 'em and Leave 'em" attitude toward sports. If I found a sport I was good at, I would do everything I could to excel in it. I was good and I knew it. It allowed me to win scholarships to several colleges, but as hard as I tried to excel under some coaches, even in the sports I liked, something didn't work. I got just so far, and then the passion turned off. The answer to why that light turned off was hidden deep inside me. I needed to find out why.

I chased those thoughts and memories out of my head and made my way to Coach Watson's class. At last I was going to meet the man I'd heard on the radio. The man who opened my life up to possibilities and put me on this campus. Yes! I was back in my element and raring to go.

Coach outlined the semester for us, handing out the syllabus, gym shorts and t-shirts with the Maryland State Hawks logo emblazoned on the front, but said we would have to wear our own gym shoes outside of class and in the field. Since this was a four-credit class, instead of the usual three credits you earn for each course passed, we were incorporating two elements into the semester—classroom instruction, and the physical anatomy of specific sports. We would take to the field or gymnasium for that part, and we would be breaking apart the teaching of wrestling and golf.

I sat on the bleacher bench in a daze. As luck would have it, the two sports I loved, Wrestling and Golf, would be the focus of my first Phys. Ed. class. Hell, it was because of my Wrestling scholarship that I got into the University of Maryland in College Park in the first place. The coach spoke of what lay in front of us, what we were expected to do, and what he expected from each of us. He spoke as eloquently in front of the group as he did on the radio. And if the coach noticed I was the only white male in the group, he never showed it.

My head was spinning as I left the Athletic building, and the smell of my bologna sandwich warming up in my book bag told me I needed to eat before I finished my classes for the day. The Student Union was just across the street and as I walked in, students were milling around, sitting at tables in groups of three or four, laughing, eating, and sharing the excitement of the first week of classes. It all stopped when I walked in.

The quiet in the room was deafening. The white guy had arrived. Word had spread that I was enrolled, and while some of the students were just getting to know me, others weren't so sure why I was there. Their eyes followed me as I pulled a soda from the bucket of ice full of sodas. I paid and sat down, alone, at one of the tables. I felt conspicuous but knew it would be a matter of time before I could blend in with the rest of the student body. Where my whiteness wouldn't be my outstanding feature.

The first few weeks of classes seemed to fly by. I had made my mind up to practice what had gotten me this far in life. I was determined to be friendly to everyone, to acknowledge a smile with a smile. Being friendly opened me up and made me accessible. And it gave me the feeling that I belonged at Maryland State College. I felt comfortable as students started saying hello as we passed between classes. Others simply nodded. Even the professors offered a friendly smile. Occasionally, Bob—the big guy who rescued me from the parking lot cop and helped me avoid a ticket—would walk by between classes and say, "What's up, white boy?" I'd walk by with a smile on my face, acknowledging his friendly jab. At least I hoped it was a friendly jab.

One day, after I had finished a class and was on my way to the Student Union, I saw Bob coming down the hall. It was like David meeting Goliath. He was tall, at least six foot six and two hundred and forty pounds or more. His arms rippled with muscles, and the elastic on the sleeves of his shirt cut into his flesh. He was so well-groomed that I felt underdressed. He smiled at everyone he passed, as they acknowledged him with friendly slaps on his arms, hand, or anywhere they could touch his giant of a body. All I had was my personality and the desire to make a friend. Before he had a chance to say, "What's up, white boy?" I said to him, "What's up, Black boy?"

He stopped dead in his tracks. There was a look of amazement and apprehension on his face. And then he smiled back at me.

I breathed a sigh of relief, knowing that if he didn't take what I had said with a degree of humor that I was dead. Perhaps even literally.

"Listen, I never thanked you for talking that cop into giving me back my car at Registration," I said. "I really appreciate that you did that." I stuck out my hand and said, "I'm Fred Engh."

He grabbed my hand, in what I could only describe as a vice-like grip, and said, "I'm Bob . . . Bob Taylor. And you're welcome."

Taking a deep breath, I then said, "I'm going to get lunch. Want to join me?"

We headed to the Student Union together. Kids in the hallways continued to greet him, while the girls all had sudden sweet smiles on their faces as we passed.

At that point, I had no idea who Bob Taylor was—given his size, however, and the fact that he wore a sweater with Maryland State athletic patches sewn all over it, it didn't take much to figure him for a football player. I remembered that the parking lot cop had referred to Bob playing football, and if I had my choice, I would never go against him on any playing field . . . ever.

The Student Union was jammed. The tables were crowded and full of students, feasting on their low-cost lunches. I brought my lunch sandwiches and fruit from home. A fellow student came over to us and pointed out an empty table, so I grabbed it while Bob went off to the hot lunch line.

"Whoa," I said, as he dropped his loaded lunch tray onto the table. Staring up at me was macaroni and cheese, meatloaf, a turkey leg, stuffing, and a huge pile of mashed potatoes and gravy along with several slices of corn bread. "That must have cost a fortune!"

"My scholarship pays for my meals. They feed me and give me a place to sleep and study in the dorm. Otherwise, no Bob!"

"Okay, fill me in. A scholarship, and full board. So why did that cop in the parking lot give in so easily when you came over? And why is everyone looking at you?"

"Maybe they're looking at you," he said, but I knew better . . . or at least I hoped I knew better.

As we sat at our table—one white guy and Bob—his apparent fan club seemed to maneuver their way through the room in order to pass Bob. I received an occasional nod and glance but felt clearly that I was invading sacred territory. "I play football for the school. That's all."

So I figured, but I had to ask, "No . . . there's gotta be more to this than you being on the football team. You must be good."

"I'd say so," he said, with an embarrassed smile crossing his face.

"Are you being scouted?" I asked, knowing that professional football scouts were like locusts when they sniffed a good college player.

His modesty impressed me. "Yeah, they've come to our games. We've got a lot of good players."

As we sat across from each other, both of us a little apprehensive at this budding relationship and playing with our food, he looked me in the eye with a serious expression on his face, and asked, "What are you doing here? You're white!"

I nearly choked on the peanut butter swimming around in my mouth, never expecting a question like that. I swallowed, giving me time to regain my composure and giving him the only answer I could: "This is the only college around that'll give me a four-year Physical Education teaching degree. I'm halfway there, but I need two more years."

I told him about turning down a Wrestling scholarship when I got out of high school, my big mistake. "I was too small to play basketball when I got to high school, so I went out for the wrestling team. I made the varsity my first year and only lost a match in the finals of the national tournament in my senior year. West Virginia offered me a wrestling scholarship."

"I'm impressed. So why didn't you go to West Virginia when they gave you the scholarship? Shit! That's a no-brainer! Man, a scholarship is a dream for any high schooler."

That was my chance to brag a bit, telling him how I captained the team as a senior. Told him how I made the All-American Prep school team. It obviously didn't impress him.

"And you threw that away?" he asked, amazed at my stupidity. Suddenly the idiocy of my younger life hit me in the face . . . again.

"I wasn't ready. Maybe I was immature. I spent the summer renting beach umbrellas to tourists in Ocean City, drinking beer, playing in a band, dating girls, and then went into the Army."

"Wait!" Bob interrupted. "Your ass was in the Army?"

"Yep, two years," I said. "Be glad you didn't have to do it. I was eighteen. If you didn't sign up for the service then, you knew that sooner or later, they'd catch up with you. I wanted to get it over with," I explained, omitting that Muzzie thought I was an idiot and a loser to put the Army ahead of college. "I went back to college at Maryland in College Park with a wrestling scholarship and the G.I. Bill—but quit that after two years."

I told him how all my free time away from the Wrestling team was spent at the driving range. "I'd finally found a sport that I really enjoyed—golf. It was, and still is, my number one game. Then one day, as I was hitting golf balls at the school driving range, I turned around. The wrestling coach was behind me. As soon as I saw him, I thought to myself, *Oh, shit, I'm in trouble.*

"The coach looked at me and said, 'Well, what do we have here? A country clubber? Look, Engh, you're on the Wrestling team—on a damn scholarship, if I have to remind you—and this is where you spend all your free time?! You need to be in the gym, practicing, and not here, wasting those scholarship dollars!' I never ever stepped into Maryland's wrestling room again. I lost my scholarship, room, and meals—all of it."

"Man, I don't get you white boys! You have the world given to you, and what do you do? Quit! Two scholarship offers, and you quit! And does hiding out at Maryland State make you any less of a quitter? Why'd you do that?"

Whoa! Only Muzzie had gone at me the way Bob did, and he didn't even know me. But he made me think. I put the sandwich down onto the table, sipped my drink, and stared at the wall before I gathered the right words to say. "I *was* a quitter. I coasted through my early years, not caring where I was going because I always believed there'd be something for me in sports if only I could find it. That's what I'm doing here."

"So, life hit you in the face and you had to grow up?"

"Had to. I've got a wife, two kids, and a little one due in the spring. It's about time."

"What're you, Catholic? Got to be. Only Catholics knock out babies one after another."

A silence hung over the table before Bob broke it by telling me something about himself. About his love of football and how it was one of the few sports that was open to Black players without the hometown breaking into riots. But he said that if he had had his choice, and if the world were different, he probably would have become a professional golfer.

"Like I told you before, golf is my number-one game! I can't believe you're telling me this," I said, and watched as a smile etched across Bob's face.

I told him how I loved playing golf, but there never was any time or money to do it.

"How good are you?" Bob asked.

"Well, the last time I played I shot seventy-seven."

"Damn, Engh, you really *can* play golf!" Bob said. "I'll tell you what . . . after football season is over, find your clubs, clean them off, and we'll talk to the coach about you playing golf on the team we're putting together. I've already talked to a few other guys about playing. We need to round out the numbers. Only one condition, though, Engh. If he gives you the go-ahead, no quitting. You got that?" Getting up from the table, he punched me in the arm. I guess that was his way of apologizing for raking me over the coals. He picked up his books, said good-bye, and walked out of the room, his entourage following close behind. I smiled as I rubbed my arm, wondering if there would be any black and blue marks from the friendly punch he had just delivered.

That was also the first time he called me by my name, and it wasn't the last. I was never going to be "white boy" to him again.

I had a friend. My first Maryland State friend, and knowing Bob made me feel confident about being in college again. About having a goal. And even Sister Angela noticed my lifted spirits as she kept adjusting my teaching schedule to accommodate my classes.

It was fall, and Maryland State was in the middle of their football season. On Saturday, with all my chores done around the trailer, I decided to go down to the college and see the home football game with Morgan State, Maryland State's top rival. Bob would be playing, and it would give me a chance to see how good he was.

The stands were filled with cheering students rooting for their teams. The Maryland State fans were all decked out in their maroon and gray school colors. Looking around, I felt like the lone matchstick in Muzzie's prank matchbook. I had read that Queen Elizabeth II had attended a football game at the College Park campus, and while there wasn't any royalty at our game, I felt as proud as I could be to be rooting for "my" school and to be surrounded by people who accepted me for who I was, not for being just the "white boy."

The game was terrific. It was obvious that both teams were well prepared and well coached. Bob was definitely a standout, but along with him there was Earl Christy and Emerson Boozer. While I may not have been a football scout, from what I could see it was obvious that these three players all had talent. By the time I came home, I was convinced that Bob and his two teammates were NFL material, and would be drafted after their senior year. With Bob, his height, strength, ability to study the field and know where he should be made him the remarkable player he was.

I ran into him a few days later, coming out of class. "Man, you tore up that field on Saturday!" I said, giving him a light punch on the arm that landed like I had hit a pile of bricks.

"You were there?" he asked, not even flinching.

We fell into step with each other and walked toward the Student Union. I liked how it seemed to be understood that we would sit at the same table during lunch. Me, with my brown bag and leftover chicken salad sandwich, and Bob with his tray loaded with practically everything they had on the food line.

I told him how the game had revved up the football juices in me and that I had a plan for the kids at the Catholic School where I taught part-time. I had always wanted to play football when I was in high school, but the wrestling coach would never allow it. He said I might get hurt; and if I did, my chances of getting a college scholarship were doomed. Finally, in my senior year, he consented, and I played for one season.

"Hey, if you need any pointers, just let me know. I'll be glad to help," he suggested.

The fun of playing football never left me. Sports was in my blood. It also gave Bob and me a lot to talk about when we ran out of golf stories to tell each other.

As the semester came to a close, exam season rolled in. Never a great test taker, I spent every waking moment that I wasn't working, studying. It's not an easy task for a guy who never read a book because of a learning disorder. My concentration was limited to a few sentences. I couldn't memorize the important facts. My spelling sucked. Understanding what I had just read took several passes to grasp even the minutest bit of information. It had been like that through all my schooling—and things had not changed much. I still struggled.

My math professor recognized the difficulty I was having and worked with me. He had worked with other students who thought math was difficult, especially since Algebra is the equivalent of translating hieroglyphics. Something in our brains has a hard time computing the problems, but by using Dr. Hytche's step-by-step approach, it suddenly became clearer. He became my hero.

He knew what I was going through, but he also recognized that I was good with the linear thinking that it took to grasp Algebra. Working together, he helped me nail the final. When I saw the letter "A" on my grade sheet, I almost fainted. He was brilliant! I was not, but he made me feel like I was. What a difference it would have made if I had had teachers like him in my high school.

While my free time was limited, between school, work, my family, and playing in the jazz band, Mike would tell me it was okay to go out with my friends. I had known them from my first two years at college and from having grown up in the area. They were my drinking buddies. And while my partying days were definitely over, we'd get together always with the blessing of Mike. A month or two after school began, my friends and I went out for a beer. I happened to mention that I was finally going to get my teaching degree. They had all graduated college and pretty much knew my story. When one of them asked me where I was going to school, I told them Maryland State College in Princess Anne. As soon as I said that, I got funny looks from all of them, followed by a few comments. "Why the hell would you want to go to a Black college? You know it can't compare to any 'white' college."

One of them even told me I was taking the easy way out by going to Maryland State. He reasoned that as a segregated college, how good could it be? Most all of the elementary, middle, and high schools in our state were either Black or white. And all the Black schools were the worst. They were underfunded, and probably had terrible teachers. That's why most of the kids going to those schools would drop out, anyway. What did that say about their school system, and what did that say about the college I was attending? Everything in those schools was inferior, they thought.

It was no secret that the public school system the Black kids were attending had problems, but none of my buddies knew anything about Maryland State. They didn't know the students or the faculty, but what they did know was that I was attending a Black college—and that's all the information they needed to know. Their judgment was cast. I could have argued with them until I was blue in the face—which I did—but the fact was that they had inherited a belief that Black people were inferior. The Civil War may have been won by the North, but the racism had never been beaten. It was still very much alive.

There was no winning the arguments I had with my friends. The fact that I could be friendly with Blacks must have put me in a very different light in their eyes because it wasn't too long afterwards that we drifted apart. But I knew that in life, as in all challenges, it's not a matter of just getting there, it's the journey that counts. My means to an end was to finish my degree, become a qualified Maryland teacher, and to look with pride at the diploma hanging proudly in my office. But my journey was going to take me to a world not many white people experience. And if I were going to lose a few "friends" on the way, so be it.

6

All About Sports

The fall semester quickly turned into spring, and my balancing act between part-time teaching, being a husband and father, playing in the band, and studying had found its equilibrium. It was also a time of growing racial discord, with the nearby town of Cambridge being the hotbed. Protestors from the local Cambridge high school, Morgan State College, and Maryland State had been mobilized, and arrests followed. While rumblings were heard all around the Maryland State campus, the fact that the disturbances were about an hour away isolated us somewhat.

I tried to stay away from talk of the racial divide as much as I could, but I could see the distress in Bob's face as we sat in the Student Union having one of our marathon lunches. Classmates stopped by our table. Whenever talks of the disturbances came up, he'd make a point by introducing me as, "my friend, Fred." I could sense their unease at seeing me with Bob, their hero, but his introduction seemed to quell whatever hostility they felt, at least for the moment.

"Did you read about Ernie Davis?" he asked. "The first Black college player to win the Heisman?" I'd read about the kid from Syracuse being voted number one and had thought about Bob as I read the report. It just proved that the walls of segregation were coming down.

"How did the Catholic kids finish up their football season?" he asked, picking up a French fry and coating it with ketchup before putting it into his mouth. He slid the French fry tray toward me, nodding that I was welcome to help myself. "Man, ketchup sure makes everything better!"

I followed his lead; not letting on that ketchup repulsed me! I launched into the story of how the nuns and parents thought I was crazy, not to mention my wife when I wanted to start a football team at the school. "You do know one of those kids could get hurt. Right?" Mike had said. "Getting hurt is part of the game" was my only reply.

One of the priests, Father Fink, thought football was a great equalizer. I made him my assistant coach. I figured I'd have the Lord on our side if one of the kids got hurt.

I had no idea what I was doing as a first-time football coach. I had to find eleven kids who would sign up for the team. And these were middle school-age kids who didn't know a football field from one end to the other. I pled with uninterested, non-athletic kids just to fill out the roster. One boy, Walter, was fifty pounds overweight. I figured he'd be a good choice for the front line. He started crying the first day and said he wanted to go home. This was going to be a tough recruiting venture.

I convinced Walter to be our waterboy by telling him I'd buy him a candy bar every day if he signed up. He did. We got our eleven. The local Salvation Army had a youth sports program and said we could have some of their old equipment. Sure enough, they let us have their old, smelly uniforms and broken-down shoulder pads. The shirts were white, so we used magic markers to put numbers on the backs.

A week later, I was on the field with my team, drawing up plays in the dirt. I was getting excited about the whole idea. I'd give them ideas picked up on the sidelines at my old high school or from watching the University of Maryland Terrapins play. A lot of them wanted to quit that first week, but I promised them an "A" in gym class if they stuck with it.

After a few weeks of practice, I even went so far as to call an area coach at a nearby middle school and challenged him to a scrimmage game. He told me he'd never even heard of our school. Hoping to get him to agree to a game, I said, "You'll know who we are after you see us play." It worked. He agreed to play us.

Everyone at the school was excited about the idea. Even the girls formed a cheerleading squad and made uniforms. They also gave the team a nickname, "The Frankies." The girls thought it was cute, naming our team after St. Francis, the Saint our school was named after.

The date was set. I was off to conquer the world with a ragtag bunch of kids. I spent almost every waking hour thinking of ways to prepare and motivate these kids. We had several practices, and some of them were pretty quick to pick up on things.

A week before our game, I decided to go to another middle school's game. Watching the formations and plays these teams were using made me feel like we might have a chance at not getting slaughtered.

I was in seventh heaven on game day, living the dream of coaching a football team. That is, until I looked across the field. There, looking like the Chicago Monsters of the Midway, in their bright red uniforms and shiny helmets, were the Seaford Lions. Surely, these players were from some local college who were lost. Images of a train wreck with bodies flying everywhere crossed my mind. Father Fink stood there with what appeared to be silent prayers coming from his lips.

Walter stood with tears in his eyes, as if preparing to be pushed over a cliff.

Dressed in our grass-stained white jerseys, dented helmets, and mismatched equipment, we were a sight to behold. I wanted to herd everyone back on to the bus and head home immediately. Embarrassment would be the least of my worries. I was fearful we would be carrying half my team to the hospital before halftime. I would be sued for all I was worth for pretending to know what I was doing. Where would Mike and the kids live when I was in jail?

The game began. One thing we had going for us was that we had a fantastic athlete, Michael Strayer—one of the fastest thirteen-year-olds you can imagine. He was our quarterback. Every play we drew up in the sand called for quarterback sneaks. We'd sneak in sweep plays that had him tearing down the sidelines for dear life. By the time we reached the fourth quarter, he'd rushed for three touchdowns against our opponents' two. The Frankies held on for the win. Visions of being the next coach of the New England Patriots and destined for the Hall of Fame crossed my mind.

Bob roared as I told my story! "Good for you, Engh! Sorry I didn't get to see one of your games, but you gave those kids something to be proud of."

The tray of French fries having been demolished, Bob pulled a few golf tees from his pocket and started lining them up in football formation on the table.

Looking at the tees, I had to ask Bob: "How did a boy from South Carolina manage to learn to play golf?"

"You mean a Black boy from South Carolina?"

"Yeah, a Black boy playing a white man's game," I said.

Bob toyed with the white tees on the table, fingering each one as he told me his story:

"When I was sixteen, living with my family in Columbia, South Carolina, we didn't have any money. No one who was Black had money. So, for us to have food on the table, everyone had to bring home some money for the day. One summer, I got a job at a golf course. I'd caddy for the rich white guys and make two or three dollars. That was a lot for me. I'd stop on the way home and get whatever my mother told me to buy from the store.

"Some days I'd stay at the course and pick up balls on the driving range. I'd watch how all the good golfers would swing their different clubs and then try to copy it. I got a chance to hit golf balls after everyone had gone home. The club never allowed us Black kids to hit on the driving range, so we'd find an iron that was left hanging around and hit balls down the fairway. We'd look all day for lost balls. Sometimes I'd have as many as fifty. A couple of cheap guys at the club would offer to buy the balls, but the club didn't like us selling them. So, we hid most of the ones we found. I'd look for drivers that were left around in the locker room and then tee up the ball and hit it as far as I could. Most times, I'd stay until the last flicker of light went down over the trees on the west end of the golf course.

"One day, I thought everyone had left and decided to sneak out on the driving range. I began to hit balls. They'd fly forever. This day one of the members decided to leave late and was standing by the clubhouse door when he spotted me hitting my driver. 'Damn, son, you can hit the ball!' he yelled. It surprised me when I turned around and saw him, and as he walked toward me, I told him I was sorry and hoped he wouldn't tell my boss. If he told the boss, that would be my last day at the course. He told me not to worry about it and suggested that I stay every night after the others were gone. He said he'd stay and give me pointers.

"We'd hit balls, and every time he'd show me what I was doing wrong. I got better and better. Then the bottom dropped out. One of the members happened to return and spotted us driving balls. The next day, the golf pro told me I was fired."

It wasn't lost on me that as Bob said this, the white tee in his hand suddenly snapped in two, the pieces falling to the table. Bob didn't skip a beat.

"As I walked out the door, he told me that because I was there practicing with one of the members, the committee decided to revoke his membership. I felt so guilty that I got this nice guy kicked out because all he was doing was helping a Black kid like me learn and appreciate the game of golf."

"Geez, I'm sorry," I said to him. "I never thought about golf in a segregated sense."

"Not many white people do. That's the world we came up in.

But things are changing. And maybe you and I can lead that parade," he said.

"What do you mean?" I asked, intrigued.

"I talked to Coach McCain about us starting up the golf team again."

"Okay, so what'd he say?"

"Well, he said that we need more good players for the team. I told him that you played and I would talk you into joining."

"Hold on," I said. "We would have a few hurdles to cross before that happens."

I thought about it for a few moments, knowing the hurdles I'd have to climb in order to make this happen. Coach McCain was behind one of the hurdles, and Mike was behind the other.

"What do you think Coach would say if a white guy wanted to join the team? I can see problems already."

"Why don't we let him make that decision," Bob said.

"Then I have another problem. No time. No money."

"You're throwing up roadblocks, man. But I might have the solution to that. I can't give you the time, but it won't cost you a thing to play! We can practice at a course in Pocomoke, and play all our matches for nothing."

My life was changing day by day. Not only was I at a school where, for the first time in my life, I was doing well in my classes, but I was friends with the "big man on campus." He just happened to be a great guy. And now I was being asked to join the golf team. The thought of playing golf, for free, and being part of a team, excited me. Now all I had to do was be charming when I walked into our trailer to convince Mike that more time away from home was going to be good for all of us. Or it just might get one of my golf irons wrapped around my neck!

I rehearsed my speech all the way home: "You know how much I love golf, honey. And this is my chance to play on a team, and to play for free." "Free" being the operative word. When we were dating, I'd told her about all the hours I'd spent in the University of Maryland library, struggling to read everything they had on golf, but I was determined. It was an addiction; the history of golf. The mechanics of the swing, everything published about golf, I'd read about as much as anyone with a learning disorder could read.

A good friend at the University introduced me to the game, and it was love at first swing. We'd go to the school's driving range and I was the pest, asking everyone in sight for pointers. We branched out to play the cheap golf courses, par-3s, executive courses, anything we could get onto for as little money as possible. But now it was different. I would have to compensate for any of my free time away from Mike and the kids by wrapping my hands around my clubs. Not easy.

I hadn't even spoken with Coach McCain yet, but Mike was the preamble. Without her okay, talking to him was pointless.

I'll say this about my wife; she's efficient. She has the house running on a schedule. Cooks. Cleans. Manages our money like a banker. And is a wonderful mother to our kids. She's also my voice of reason whenever I run a crazy idea past her. Going to Maryland State was one of them. Playing golf was another.

Yes, Mike didn't like the idea of me riding around the countryside, traveling to matches in a car filled with Black people. She didn't like the idea of my "white" matchstick possibly getting burned. And she didn't know if the coach would warm to the idea of a white boy playing on the team. And what teams would we be playing—all Black, or mixed? But she also knew that playing golf for a few months would take the edge off my constantly running to teach, running to play in the band, running to the library to study when the noise in the house got too much. The only thing she asked of me, the same thing she asked when I told her of my idea of going to Maryland State, was that if I felt threatened I'd stuff my clubs into the bag and come home.

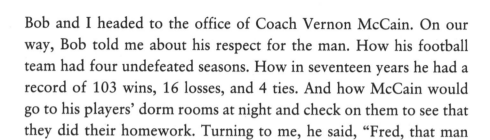

Bob and I headed to the office of Coach Vernon McCain. On our way, Bob told me about his respect for the man. How his football team had four undefeated seasons. How in seventeen years he had a record of 103 wins, 16 losses, and 4 ties. And how McCain would go to his players' dorm rooms at night and check on them to see that they did their homework. Turning to me, he said, "Fred, that man is responsible for who I am today."

Walking into the coach's domain, I was nervous, but his warm handshake immediately put me at ease as he said that Coach Watson, the head of the Physical Education department, had told him about me. The "white kid," as he called me. *At least they knew who I was,* I thought to myself. He then introduced me to Ted Briggs, the golf coach who had been invited to come into the meeting. I felt like I was in an inquisition, with both coaches staring at me.

"Sit down, *both* of you," McCain directed Bob and me, as we moved into a conversation about the golf team, its past history, and where he wanted to take it that year. He mentioned that Bob worked his way up to being the number one player on the team, and that the other three players were right behind him.

I looked across at Bob and gave him a friendly smile, knowing how much golf meant to him and the acknowledgement the coach was giving him.

Coach Briggs then asked if I thought I could compete on their level. He asked about my interest in golf and if I could commit to the time it took, practicing and playing, during the season. Would it interfere with my studies, my family, my work? I felt like I was in friendly fire, but as the questions flowed, I grew to understand the seriousness of these men and their commitment to the game.

Briggs then told us that this may be the team's last season and asked if I was still interested if it meant playing for only a few months.

I told him I would play if it were the last week of the season, that's how much I loved golf!

Bob had also spoken to Coach Briggs and had told him about my time at the University of Maryland, and about my scores the last few rounds I'd played. "Well, we need a good golfer on the team," Briggs remarked. "Think you can play your way up to the number two spot?" he asked.

It was my turn to talk. I told him I did play golf at the College Park campus, but I could not be on the golf team because I was on a scholarship to the Wrestling team, so the closest I could get to the golf team was watching them tee-off at their matches. I watched them practice, and I watched them on the driving range. The same driving range where I went every day after class, and where I would hit balls for hours. I assured them that I hoped to be good enough to qualify for their team.

I told both coaches that, for the most part, I shot in the high 70s, low 80s, but must have sounded nervous when I asked about the scheduled matches, and where they would be played. I also broached the subject of my skin color being a problem. Would the other players on the team resent me for it? Would it cause trouble when we had to travel for matches? Both men assured me that anyone giving me trouble would be dealt with. Coach Briggs handed me a play schedule and said, "I'd like to welcome you to our team." On the basis of having Bob vouch for me, and that my golfing scores were impressive, I was officially a member of the Maryland State Hawks' golf team and was told matches would begin in April.

Walking to my car after the meeting, I was exhilarated. I asked Bob, "How did you manage to get to 'number one' on the golf team, especially after being banged around on the football field for months before?"

"Fred, I worked hard for that position, just as I've worked hard every day of my life to gain respect from teachers, coaches, and teammates. It's not easy when you come from where I do, and I expect you to do the same and earn your way up to 'number two.'"

"Yes, sir!" I said, giving him a salute—then I happened to look at the schedule I was given. I stopped dead in my tracks. All of our matches were going to be played against all-Black colleges in the Maryland, Delaware, Virginia triangle, where a white man could get in big trouble if he was seen hanging around with Black players.

"Bob, as a Black golf team—now with one white guy, of course— will golf courses allow a mixed Black-and-white team to play? And where could we practice?" I asked, cautiously.

"First of all," Bob replied, "the teams we play come from other Black colleges. Second, over the years the schools have made arrangements allowing us to play on local public courses. It's not like our matches don't get noticed when we play, but we have as much of a right to be on the public courses as any of the other white players."

"And you don't run into any problems playing there?" I questioned.

"Sometimes. But I don't let it get into my head or interfere with my game. And that's my word of advice, for now."

I knew I had work to do—not only on my physical game but my mental game as well. It was going to be a challenge; but if Bob could do it, so could I. I didn't want to lose the respect of the coaches who were taking a bet on me. More important, I couldn't lose Bob's respect.

7

The Course Ahead

A week later, I got a phone call from Coach Briggs saying we would be having a meeting for the golf team on Saturday morning. When I arrived at his office, Bob Taylor was in conversation with three other young men who I assumed were the other members of the team. You could almost see their jaws dropping as they stopped talking and looked me over. Bob interrupted the silence, putting his arm around my shoulder and introducing me to Eugene, Joey, and Oscar—players who rounded out the team.

Coach Briggs said that since I was the only new guy on the team, it would be up to Bob to fill me in on how we operated, our responsibilities, and the importance of keeping our spirits high and our scores low.

The coach asked us to sit, and then launched into his inaugural team talk while Bob took the chair next to mine. He leaned over and, in a very low voice, said, "Looks like you and I are going to have to bear the load for the team. Hope you're as good as you said you were!" I wasn't intimidated. I was scared shitless!

Coach Briggs continued. "What I'm going to say isn't new to you who were on the team before, but for Fred's sake, and to refresh your memories, be aware that your practice score before the match determines your playing position the day of the match. Get out there on a course, play as often as you can, and bring your best play to the practice round. We play as a team, you each have your strengths and in the end those strengths will add up to a winning season."

All of us sat there, our heads nodding in agreement, trying to get psyched. But in golf, the coaches don't do the psyching up, the players have to bring it to the course themselves. You're in charge. No one is telling you how you can and can't play. Control is in your hands, and more importantly, in your head.

Coach then went on: "Charlie Sifford just broke through the color wall on the PGA tour. Let's get your games on and follow him through that wall. As Dr. Martin Luther King said when he spoke here at our graduation ceremony three years ago, 'Doors are opening today that were not opened yesterday. The challenge of this hour is to be ready to enter these doors when they open.'"

Coach Briggs continued the meeting by telling us that all our matches will be away at other colleges within a two-hour drive, and before our first match we were to practice not only as a team but whenever our schedules would allow.

In the meantime, he had gotten permission from the Winter Quarters golf course in Pocomoke, a few miles away from the campus, for us to practice. While I had never heard of Winter Quarters golf course, I was excited to finally get a chance to play, and it would not cost me a penny. The coach then told us that practice would begin on the following Saturday, and we were expected to show up at nine A.M. The first team order would be determined by the scores each player posted at the end of the round. I felt confident and ready to show them I could play.

I left the trailer park at seven that Saturday morning. I had been to Pocomoke several times, but not to Winter Quarters. When I got to town, I needed to ask a few folks where the course was. After driving around in search of something that resembled a golf course, I spotted what looked to be one nestled among a group of typical looking small family homes.

I parked the car and started to walk around to make sure what I was looking at was, in fact, an eighteen-hole course. There in front of me was a sign indicating this was *The Winter Quarters*. While my time on regular golf courses may have been limited, this one did not seem to look like any golf course I had ever been on. The map posted next to the sign referred to it as an eighteen-hole course but showed only nine holes. I guess if you played it twice around, you would get the eighteen holes. I'm not sure how the United States Golf Association would have rated the course, but let's say it would have been a challenge. And by challenge, I mean trying to determine where the fairway started and ended. Most of the grass was gone, and where there was no grass, sand took its place. Not exactly what I was expecting, but it was going to be the place we could practice, and it would be free.

I walked into the pro shop and sitting in the corner were four middle-aged locals, looking like they were more about fishing than golfing. At that time, when a stranger, regardless of his skin color, walked into a room on the Eastern Shore of Maryland, the locals would look at him like he was some weird creature invading their space. Something like being an alien.

I told them I was with the Maryland State College golf team, and here to practice. "Is this where I sign in?"

"You gotta be *shittin'* me!" said one of the men dressed in baggy jeans and an overly worn tee-shirt that read *I Love Harleys* across the front.

The first thing that came out of one of the other men's mouth was asking how the hell I was on a golf team from that Black school. The others in the group began to laugh as he went on to say, "By the looks of things, you *appear* to be white." At that very moment, I appreciated even more the idea of Bob Taylor being on our team. If I used the phrase "a bone-chilling figure of intimidation" to describe Bob, that might *still* have been an understatement. And no sooner had these guys finished their laughing, than Bob and the other three players on the team entered the front door. There was a silence in the room that was deafening. Coach Briggs stood in the doorway and told the startled group that the local golf pro said we were scheduled to tee off now. As the six of us walked out the door toward the course, I turned and said to the four in the corner, "I guess I *really* look white to you now."

In golf, it is customary for four players to tee off at the same time. Coach Briggs decided that since we were the only ones playing on the course at that time, all five of us could play together. "That way," he said, "I can easily evaluate your play, and determine the ranking for the team."

In a matter of minutes, it was clear that we didn't need to have a tryout to see who would be number one on the team. I had seen the top-notch college golfers at the College Park campus. Players like Deane Beman, who went on to win the U.S. Amateur, were among the best in the nation. When I saw Bob Taylor hit his first drive, I was impressed! He had all the fundamentals of an outstanding golfer. *Yes! This is going to be fun,* I thought, as a smile swept across my face.

"Not bad for a football player! I guess you haven't lost it," Eugene cried out, shaking his head in wonder at the 300-yard, straight-down-the-middle drive that Bob had just executed. I was last to tee up and all eyes were on me, as if I had to prove myself— which, in fact, I did. I took a few practice swings then put the head of my driver smack into the arch of the golf ball and watched as it soared across what was supposed to be a lush green fairway. And while it certainly was not as far as the ball Bob had hit, it had enough distance as it sailed straight down the center of the fairway, farther than anyone else except Bob had hit. Joey, Eugene, and Oscar stood there quietly being both impressed and, I guess, disappointed. And after playing a few holes, the coach made it clear that I had solidified my place on the team.

After practice, Coach Briggs called Bob and me to the side and said, "It looks like the two of you are going to be 'One' and 'Two' on this team. Joey, Eugene, and Oscar definitely need to put in some practice time, but if we can bring their games up, we could have quite a season."

For most athletic teams, practice is paramount. Our golf team at Maryland State College was not your average college athletic team. In fairness, Bob and I were the only two real golfers on the team. So it made sense that the two of us would practice, or should I say, just play golf whenever we got the chance. Mostly that would be on Saturdays when a match wasn't scheduled.

There used to be a cartoon character in the comic strips called "Mr. Milquetoast." He was a timid old soul, afraid of everything. That was me on Saturday mornings, when I would approach my wife, Mike, and say sheepishly, "Do you mind if Bob and I go practice today?"

Like I've said before, there's nothing like having a wife who doesn't nag at you for not tending to "honey-do" lists on a Saturday morning—especially when it's seventy degrees and sunny outside, and the golf course beckons.

Bob and I had a plan for our Saturday "play" dates. He would wait for the "All Clear" call from me and knew that within a half-hour we'd both be heading for Pocomoke. I'd drive south to the school, pick him up, and on the way we'd joke that we were heading for one of the world's great golf courses "to practice." That being the Winter Quarters Golf Club—the pride of Pocomoke, Maryland. As spring wore on, grass on Winter Quarters was as hard to find as the grass on the Sahara Desert. But hey, it was a place to hit a golf ball around.

Little did I know that at the end of this day it would be more about something I would never have dreamt would come to be for me—the beginning of a friendship, unlike any I'd ever known. Me, and a Black guy.

On our way to Pocomoke, Bob suggested that we play for the right to see who would be number one on the team. Always being up for a challenge, I said, "You're on."

One thing about golf that the old-timers used to say was, "You can learn more about a person in one round of golf than you can at a year of cocktail parties." That was certainly true of Bob and me. While we may have become friends over lunch in the cafeteria, playing a sport together and being on a team would make us that much closer over time. Close enough to have him trash-talking about my game, which is what a lot of athletes do. They try to rattle you. To push you forward. To improve your game. Bob would say to me, "You're good, but Engh, you are lazy . . . You gotta follow through on all your swings." He used it to get to me. Still, in spite of the way it came out, he taught me a lot about golf, and surprisingly, much more. I think the fact I could take criticism so easily impressed Bob, too. He laughed and said, "Bring it on, brother."

Hole after hole, we walked the course. He would outdrive me by fifty yards. He would chip better than me. When it came to putting, I was better than him, and he would get mad at missing putts. All along, as we played, the maintenance guy hovered menacingly behind us on his tractor, following us on each hole. By the scowl on his face, I was sure he didn't like the idea of Bob—a Black guy—playing with this white man on "his" golf course.

Bob and I both hit our shots into a sand trap on the seventh hole, hit our balls out onto the green ahead, putted, and moved on to the next hole.

Suddenly, the maintenance guy turned his tractor toward us, driving at a speed that put us both on edge. Slamming on his brakes just a few inches in front of us and with a threatening look on his face, he looked at Bob and said, "Boy, let me tell you something! On this golf course, we rake the bunker after hitting out of it. You git that?"

Calling a Black man "boy" was by then a clearly established way to degrade and knock at a man's spirit. I was shocked when Bob never said a word as he looked straight ahead. He simply said, "Yes, sir."

I was dumbfounded. I thought, here's a giant of a guy, who in the autumn could crash through offensive lines and throw running backs to the ground with fury. He had the right to grab the guy off the tractor and throw him to the ground the same way. But he didn't. He was calm beyond belief.

I was not. I lost control and started toward the maintenance man, my seven iron firmly gripped in my hand and anger written on my face. Bob grabbed me by the arm saying, "Don't. You're not going to change his way of thinking. Believe me, I've been through this before."

Bob slowly walked back to the trap, picked up the rake, and put the sand back in place. I stood next to the maintenance man, the head of my club bouncing in my hand, a silent threat. His eyes were fixed on Bob and under his breath I thought I heard him mumble these words—"Fuckin' n - - - - r. Shouldn't be out here, anyway." He turned around, looked at me, and said, "You ain't no better." He then sped off, leaving tire tracks in the fairway.

As we walked toward the next tee, Bob turned to me and lamented, "Now you know what it feels like to grow up in the south, Engh." I stood there motionless, wondering what had just happened. Still angry, I said to myself, "That bastard hasn't heard the last from me."

It was perhaps the first time I felt the difference between being Black and white.

When I looked at Bob, I no longer saw the Black man who jokingly called me white boy. I only saw a friend.

From that day on, I had a new perception of not only Bob, but my fellow classmates at Maryland State. It was likely that they all had to put up with this maintenance guy's kind of attitude all their lives. When I entered Maryland State College, I had a single purpose. It was to graduate from college. I didn't go there to break any barriers by being a white guy at an all-Black college. I just wanted my degree. I wanted to get on with life. But now, I was a person who understood that the students I went to class with had to suffer the indignities of white people their entire lives. Beyond the walls of Maryland State College, they would be made to feel less than equal to their white counterparts. No eating at counters, no going to the same restrooms, no drinking from the same water fountains. How could I not feel their injustices, their abuses, their dishonor? The problem was I could not. I was white and I hadn't paid enough attention. What I did feel was shame.

On the Friday before our first match, Coach Briggs contacted all the players, saying we were to meet in his office at 4 PM. Walking in, I noticed an older looking white guy sitting in the corner, a camera in his hand. Coach introduced the man as a reporter from the *Salisbury Times* newspaper, and said he wanted to take a photo of our team. My chest shot out with pride, knowing that not only was I a college student on the golf team, but the paper wanted our picture. I was living the life!

After the photoshoot, I asked Coach Briggs if that was something the paper did every year. He said no, it was the first time, at least for the golf team. I thought to myself, *Why would they want a photo of our team before we even played our first match?* Then it dawned on me. Those rednecks from Pokomoke must have tipped the paper off that there was a white player on Maryland State's golf team. They wanted to make a story out of it—out of me. With all that was going on related to integration throughout the south, maybe they thought it would be funny to show how a white person chose to integrate a Black school. That image of the matchsticks Muzzie had given me flashed in front of me. But at that point it was too late to do anything about it anyway.

After the photoshoot, Coach Briggs announced that the five of us would have to drive up to Baltimore early Saturday morning in one of the player's car. He was going up the day before and would meet us at the course. The team was to meet on campus and figure out who was going to drive to the course. Once again, that damn image of the matchsticks popped into my head. But this time it wasn't about being seen in a newspaper. It was about being the only white person in a car full of my fellow teammates, who were all Black.

Why would I ever even think that? And as I thought about it, I realized that in all my life I had never shared a car ride with a Black person. In the army, some of the buses we rode on had a mix of Blacks and whites, but each group tended to stick together. It had never dawned on me that this would be a problem. For whatever reason, I felt uncomfortable. Maybe I had inherited more of Muzzie's attitude than I had ever imagined. My mind started whirring, trying to come up with an excuse not to drive with the team.

Bob must have noticed my concern. "What's a matter, Engh? You afraid to ride up to Baltimore with us four Blacks?" he said, laughing. "You look like you saw a ghost."

I was somewhere between embarrassed, shocked, ashamed, and a multitude of other emotions, but didn't have anyone else to blame but myself. I had decided to go to an all-Black school and to play on their golf team. Now I had to follow through. Whatever was going through my head, I was not going to let it get the best of me. Since the "boy" incident I felt more determined than ever to never let racial bias rule over me. I turned things around by telling Bob and the others that I'd be happy for all of us to travel as a team.

One thing about Bob, he may have been joking around, but I knew he sensed in me the same fear he had experienced in his life as a Black boy in the South. Except now, the tables were turned.

My mind was racing a mile a minute while driving home from the team meeting. I might have said yes to the ride, but it still didn't feel comfortable. Is this why schools and neighborhoods were segregated? Because people felt comfortable with their own kind? I didn't feel that way going to Maryland State at this point, but I wondered if the other students were comfortable seeing me there.

In less than twenty-four hours, I would be riding down the highway with four Black guys dressed like they were going somewhere important, with lily-white me sitting right there with them. This was in the '60s. I would never have dreamt of seeing a white person dare to be in a car with Black people when growing up. Word would have been all over town. How was I to be brave when every mile along the way someone would ride by and see us. What about having to stop for gas, or better yet, food?

When I got home, I asked Mike if she would like to go out for the evening. I needed something to calm my nerves, and Mike sensed that. The local burger joint was about all we could afford, and the thought of their chocolate ice cream cake for dessert was exactly what I needed at that moment. Mary Ellen, a local girl who lived in our trailer park, agreed to babysit, and off we went. It was our first date in a long time, and both of us were excited at what the present held and where we were going for our future. Strangely, the subject of golf never came up. Partly, I'm sure, was my fear of telling Mike that I would be riding with four Black guys in a car to the match in Baltimore the next day.

The trailer park was dimly lit that night as we drove home in our old green sedan, thumping into every pothole leading to the pad that held our twelve-foot wide tin can. That's what my wife and I had called our home for over three years. Home. Until I could find a way out of that trailer park. But that didn't seem likely to be anytime soon. I was enjoying my classes, teaching at the Catholic School, playing occasional gigs with Lynn's band, and studying. I was spending my days getting an education surrounded by Black kids and being taught by Black professors. I returned to my white world as soon as I left campus, which consisted of being a dad, a husband, socializing, and playing cards with my white friends.

On our ride home from dinner, we talked about how our life had changed in the past few months. We were on a mission, headed for a life with purpose. Our light mood was broken when we saw

Mary Ellen standing in front of our open door, her arms frantically waving us down. Tucked behind her, holding onto her legs as if her life depended on it, was our daughter, Kathi, fright etched across her face.

Mike immediately went into panic mode. Nothing usually phased her unless it had something to do with our kids, but seeing Kathi's little face hidden behind Mary Ellen did it.

"Oh, my God. What's going on?" Mike hollered out in her panic-stricken voice as she threw open the car door. "Mary Ellen, is everyone all right?"

The words spilled out of Mary Ellen's mouth like lava flowing from a volcano. "A man . . . a big, really big Black man came knocking at the door. Scared the heck out of us, he knocked so loud. He was looking for you!"

Mike's eyes widened. For the first time, I could read her fear as she grabbed and hugged our daughter. I quietly asked Mary Ellen if the man identified himself.

"Yes," she trembled. "Said his name was Bob Taylor!"

"Okay, Mary Ellen," I said to her in a calm voice, reassuring all of them, "Bob's a friend. He probably just stopped by to talk about our golf match tomorrow. No need to worry."

As I walked Mary Ellen home to her trailer, I told her a little bit about my being a student at Maryland State and the golf team that I was on. She didn't say much, just nodded, trying to get her head around all the jibberish I was crowding into her teen-age mind. I then wondered to myself, how would she have reacted if Bob were "some white guy?"

8

In the Rough

Mike shook me awake early the next morning, waving the *Salisbury Times* frantically in my face. There on the front page of the sports section was a picture of the Maryland State College golf team, my four Black teammates—and me.

"Shit."

Mike wasn't in the mood for any light conversation, as she glared at the photo with the rest of the team and me. Of course, everyone on the Eastern Shore reads the *Salisbury Times*. No wonder they wanted to take the photo and show me with the rest of the team. Maybe it would sell more papers. Whatever reason they chose to run that picture, there it was, and it was not sitting very well with Mike.

Trying to avoid the coming storm, I said jokingly, "Wow! I came out pretty sexy, don't you think?"

It didn't work.

"I'll tell you what I think!" she began. "I have no problem with your going to Maryland State to get your degree. I accepted the fact that you wanted to join the golf team, and that I rarely ever see you . . . but what I *don't* appreciate is your friend scaring the living daylights out of our babysitter, or that the rest of the world now knows you are going to a 'Black' college. The only people who knew were our families—but now, *everyone* knows. Our friends, our neighbors, the milkman . . . everyone!"

It wasn't that I didn't understand her reaction. I hadn't mentioned that the newspaper might be running that photo, so I could see that it might have come as a surprise. My own reaction to being

85

told I was going to the golf match in a car with my other my Black teammates was not all that different from hers. Your first reaction is to think this isn't right. If someone sees me with a Black person, I should feel embarrassed or that I'm doing something wrong.

The fact is I was doing nothing wrong. I have a right to choose whoever I want to be standing next to or be friends with, no matter what color their skin is. Now all I had to do was tell Mike how I felt, or at least how I was coming around to feeling.

I spoke to Mike about exactly that. How I became aware of how segregated the world we lived in was. How the people I went to school with were absolutely no different from any of the people we knew. And how Bob Taylor, the guy who came around the night before, was a good friend. And that, however bad she thought that picture in the newspaper was, all it showed was a picture of a golf team. And if we were going to raise our children right, that needed to be a lesson they had to learn. I was growing from the day the maintenance man called Bob "boy," and I didn't like what I had heard.

"I know how hard it must be on you to have stood by me all this time," I said. "I know how crazy this must be for you to see that picture, but that picture represents the person I want to be. The future I hope I can give you. I know I'm not perfect—sexy, yes, but not perfect. So please, if you can find it in your heart, just let it go."

As we looked at each other in this tender moment, we heard the sound of a car horn honking outside our trailer, loud enough to end the conversation and wake little Kathi.

I opened the trailer door to see who it was, and there, standing in front of the car door, stood Bob. "We're here a little early," he said, "hope I didn't wake you up."

"Give me a few minutes to get ready, and I'll be out," I said.

I walked back into the trailer, got my clubs, and gave Mike a kiss. "Wish us luck," I said. She looked at me holding Kathi, and said, "You know I do."

Having been there the night before, Bob had driven straight to our driveway without any problems. As I walked to get into the car, I couldn't help but notice all the faces peering out of other trailer windows around us, probably wondering what all those Black guys wanted. I wondered if that was why Bob chose to honk, instead of just knocking on the door.

"Good morning, Fred," he said. He then asked me if I was okay, having seen the newspaper himself. He told me he had stopped by our trailer the night before and apologized for scaring the crap out of our babysitter. I had to laugh, telling him the day had not started out the way I had expected.

"You didn't look at all happy when the coach said we were driving to Baltimore together. Are you still okay with all this?" Bob asked.

"Yeah, sure."

"You're not quitting on me, are you?"

"I gave you my promise. I will be there for you and the other guys." And with that, he hung his big Black arm around my puny white shoulders, and we walked to the car together.

We took off for Baltimore, leaving behind questioning eyes. Joey and Oscar were still laughing at their sudden celebrity, but only Eugene was quiet, and I wondered how all this was affecting him. After driving for an hour or so, we reached the town of Cambridge. This is when I got a little nervous.

Racial tensions had been building in Cambridge from when the Philips Packing plant had closed not long before. It had employed close to 10,000 people in and around Cambridge. For some reason, the white former employees felt the need to blame someone for the plant's demise. They blamed it on the local Black community; or, as they thoughtlessly referred to them, "The Coloreds."

We had passed a bus loaded with Black kids, and the signs hanging in the bus window told us they were part of the Student Nonviolent Coordinating Committee. Freedom Riders were headed into segregated Eastern Shore towns. Cambridge's white side had chosen to keep things the way they had been for an umpteen number of years. Different schools for each race.

I wanted to get out of town ASAP, but Joey, our driver, announced we needed to stop for gas. I gasped. Bob was riding shotgun. I was sandwiched in the back, between Eugene and Oscar.

Oh no, I thought. *Not now. Not here in Cambridge.* It was the feeling one might get when swimming in the ocean and realizing a school of sharks has surrounded you.

As we neared the closest gas station in Cambridge, my feelings intensified. I'm not sure why I did, but I asked Joey to stop and let me drive before we pulled in to the station. It proved to be a smart move. As we approached the station, there, out in front sat a few white roughnecks looking bored to death. Our little group couldn't have been a better target for someone wanting to punish a few Blacks and start trouble.

As we pulled up to the gas tanks, no one wanted to get out. I don't know where I got the nerve, but I got out of the car to ask for gas. When the station attendant approached, he glanced inside and saw my four Black teammates and yelled. "Holy shit! There are four n - - - - rs in the car with this white boy!"

With that, four rednecks came running up to the car and yelled, "What the hell are those n - - - - rs doing in that car?" Fearing for my life, I suddenly remembered the story about the Black golfer, Charlie Sifford. Charlie had been in a similar situation—only in reverse. He had told the sheriffs who confronted him that he had been driving his white passenger home.

I saw that Bob was starting to get agitated but signaled to him to stay in the car.

I said to the mob surrounding the car, "Oh, don't worry, guys. I'm taking these Black guys here back to Baltimore, where they work the grounds over at the baseball stadium. So they're fine, and there won't be any trouble. No need to worry."

The attendant looked us over, not quite believing my story, and said we'd better be telling the truth, and not heading for the demonstrations in town, because if we were, he'd have to drag us out of the car and beat the living piss out of all of us.

I guess we didn't look like agitators, and never taking his eyes off of us, he filled the tank and took my money.

Little did the gas station attendant know that one of my passengers to whom he referred was a six-foot-four, two-hundred-and-fifty-pound guy, who would have easily kicked all of their asses all over Cambridge.

With the car full of gas, the five of us took off again for Baltimore.

"You handled that bullshit pretty well," Bob said, patting me on the back as we headed out of town. I drove the rest of the way to Baltimore.

"So, this is the kind of crap you guys have to live with every day?" I said, shaking my head.

I was excited to play at Morgan State College. It was one of several Black colleges located in the Baltimore, Maryland area. They were our first golfing opponent and rumor had it that they were the favorite to win the Conference Championship. This would be my first test of being the white golfer on a Black college team. I worried how the other team would accept—or reject—me.

As we drove onto the College campus, we headed toward the gymnasium where we were to meet the other team's coach. All of a sudden, as we neared the gym, Bob let out a yell, "Holy shit, there's Big Daddy Lipscomb!" Big Daddy wasn't called "Big Daddy" for nothing. He stood about 6-foot and 8-inches tall and weighed well over 300 pounds. He played for the Baltimore Colts football team, and he was good. Apparently, he worked out at the Morgan State campus during the off-season. As we got out of the car, I saw Big Daddy's eyes light up as if he were seeing a long lost friend. And then he shouted out, "Who the hell is that little honkey ridin' with y'all?" He had great intensity in his voice as he glared at me. That definitely got my attention, knowing that statement was directed at me. I froze in place.

I had no idea if he was joking or just didn't like the idea of four Black guys allowing me to ride with them in the car. I was more than relieved when Bob went right over to him and said a few words that turned Big Daddy's glare into a smile. I don't know what Bob said, and I was a little too distracted to ask, but whatever it was, it did the trick. I hoped this wasn't how the rest of the day was going to go. Forget about golf. I was now in what felt like enemy territory. But Bob was my protection. We were now friends, and I knew if any trouble began, he would be there for me.

In about ten minutes, the Morgan State coach arrived. As soon as he spotted me, he said, with a questioning voice, "So, who are *you?*"

"I'm a member of the golf team at Maryland State." As the words came out, I felt an uneasiness that I hadn't expected.

"You go to Maryland State?" the coach asked. "I've never heard of a white person going to Maryland State, let alone someone playing on one of their sports teams. So is this some kind of joke or what?"

At that moment, Coach Briggs pulled up in his car and—seeing me talk to the Morgan State coach—he may have sensed that there might be some issue at hand. As he approached the group, Coach Briggs asked the other coach, "We have a problem here?"

"This white guy tells me he's a member of your team," the Morgan State coach yelled. "How's that possible? You trying to play some kind of trick on me, Coach? Like bringing in a ringer?"

Briggs said to him, "I know what you're thinking, Coach, but he's legit. He's enrolled in our school, he tried out for the team, and he made it. Is that a problem?"

As I listened to the two coaches hassle one another over me, I thought to myself, *Damn, this coach doesn't want me to play golf just because of the color of my skin. How strange is that?*

And it wasn't that I didn't understand. I could see Coach Briggs getting somewhat heated. He said, "Look, every student on your team is here because he can play a good game of golf. That's exactly how I put my team together. Imagine if you were a white coach with a white team, and I showed up with my white team and one Black player. What would your attitude about me be then? You get my drift?" Coach Briggs went on to say, "Look, if you think this white boy has an advantage then I suggest you look at the score of our number one Black player when the match is over."

I was thankful that the coach had stood up for me, but I also understood where the other coach was coming from. It wasn't anything personal, it was just how much I stood out from any of the players. Bob walked up to me and said, "Not much fun being on the receiving end, huh? Look, don't let this rattle you. Shake it off and don't be lazy! You got a match to concentrate on."

When we arrived at the Mount Pleasant Public Golf Course there were no spectators, Black *or* white. High school and college golf teams were allowed to compete on public courses, and they were scheduled in the afternoons after the regular morning golfers had finished their rounds. Sure, we got a few stares as we walked through the clubhouse on our way to the tee, but we went one way, and the early players went out the door to their cars, a few heads shaking, but no comments were made. At least that we could hear.

Since there were five golfers on each team, the coaches agreed to have two members of each team play as a foursome. The fifth players would play as a team of two. As we approached the first tee, I noticed both coaches planned to follow Bob and me around the course. I figured they still weren't over their disagreement about me playing. Or maybe they decided to place a side wager on which team would win.

For some reason, having someone watch me play fired me up. And I wanted so badly to beat my opponent. I wanted the Morgan State coach to get pissed when he saw me clobber my opponent.

I was sure Bob would do the same. Throughout the match, Bob would lean toward me and say, "We're kicking their ass." And we did. As I looked at the Morgan State coach, I could see his head was still shaking as we walked from the eighteenth green back to the clubhouse. Bob had the top score and I came in second.

Jubilation reigned as we drove down the road, back to Salisbury. Even Eugene had a smile on his face as the rhythmic pulse of jazz bassist Ray Brown's playing on Dizzy Gillespie's "Two Bass Hit" echoed from the radio while *three* sets of hands accompanied the music from the back seat. "Ray Brown's one of the great bass guitar players," I said, as I drove through the countryside with my very own golf-playing rhythm section there beside me. "My playing sucks, compared to his."

"You play bass?" Eugene asked.

"Sure do," I said.

I turned down the volume on the radio and told them about when my brother, Lynn, bought me a dinged-up bass when I was sixteen. He said that since music runs in our family veins, I had to learn how to play it. Lynn gave me lessons when he had the time, but I learned mostly by picking out my part while listening to other jazz players. It took me a while before I had the confidence to ask if I could play in his band, and he only took a chance on me when his bass player moved to Kentucky. Once in, though, I continued to play with them at lounges, bars, hotels, and even beach parties. We were getting a name for ourselves, and requests for us to play at gigs were coming in at a brisk pace.

"That's how I can afford to go to college and still feed my family. I've been playing for almost five years now. You guys aren't the only ones who can play jazz music, even if you *did* invent it," I said with a smile.

"But we're the ones who got it all going here in this country," Joey shouted from the back seat.

"I'd have to agree with you there," I yelled back over the music.

"We have two Black guys in the band. Dave and Chris. Man, are they great musicians. One plays sax, and the other guitar. Ever been to Johnny's in Salisbury? I get on stage there every once in a while, after hours."

"Wait a minute! You, a white guy, play in Johnny's? I'm surprised they even let you in," Oscar commented.

"You'll be surprised who'll let me in! Let me tell you a story," I said. "After Dave and Chris heard I was going to go to Maryland State, they thought I should experience a Black 'after hours' club. Just to get me into the swing of things. So off we went.

"Chris assured me there wouldn't be a problem. Everyone likes good music. Doesn't matter what color their skin is. Chris spoke to the club manager—and the next thing I knew, we were asked to play a few sets.

"And that, my friends, is how I got to play at Johnny's 'After Hours' Nightclub!"

"You're just lucky Morgan State's coach wasn't the manager there, or you would have been playing on the sidewalk," Oscar continued.

"Funny, but I'll tell you something that pissed me off. When we finished playing, everyone was hungry. Playing music for the night makes you feel like sitting down and having something to eat. But there was nowhere the five of us could go. Every place at that time of night was for 'Whites Only.'"

"Nothing's changed, has it?" Eugene said from the back seat. I watched through the mirror as my three teammates shook their heads in quiet resignation. It was something that must have been all too familiar to everyone in the car, but me.

We crossed the Chesapeake Bay Bridge connecting urban western Maryland with the rural Eastern Shore and drove through miles of farmlands. The open fields on the side of the road heaving with newly grown vegetables were still feeding the people of Maryland. The guys in the back seat were all looking intently at the Black field workers bent over the crops and picking their hands raw. "Only three generations back," Oscar said, "and it's likely that our ancestors may have been the ones out there working these same fields as slaves."

"Hell, I still got family working the fields in South Carolina," Bob said. "If it hadn't been for football . . . and my Mama, I'd probably be there too," he said wistfully. I felt like I could hear Bob thinking to himself, *Golf is what I like to do, but football is what I have to do.*

"Mama always told me that Black kids have the deck stacked against them, and their best weapon was to become a good athlete. 'That's your way out of here,' she'd say. 'But remember, Bobby, to keep your smarts about you. Don't let anyone get the better of you,' and she'd say it like she had preached it at church."

"Your mom sounds like a very smart lady," I said.

"And man, that woman can cook!" Bob responded.

"Yeah, and you can eat! Just look at you!" cracked Joey, as the back seat erupted in laughter.

That got me wondering. I thought about how Bob's mother told him what he needed to do to get ahead, and what Muzzie told me. Two women whose shared common goal was to see that their children had a better life. And yet, one would never want the other to be their neighbor.

9

Bonding

It was ten P.M. by the time I drove Joey's car into our trailer park. He, Eugene, and Oscar had nodded off in the back seat while Bob sat up front with me talking about each hole, each play, and what we both needed to do to up our game for the next match.

I pulled directly in front of my trailer, woke the guys in the back seat, and we all unfolded ourselves and got out of the car, welcoming the fresh air. The excitement of winning our first match, along with Joey ribbing me about being their chauffeur, increased the noise level in the neighborhood as some of the window shutters opened to see what the commotion was about. I waved to whoever was looking—hoping that no one would call the cops—and then noticed Mike's face peering out the window. I waved at her and motioned for her to come out.

Mike was a little hesitant as she climbed down the front steps, but I drew her close to me and said, "Mike, this is my golf team." After introducing all the guys, I said, "Gentlemen, this is my very understanding wife, Mike."

"Very nice to meet all of you." She then looked at Bob and said, "I think we almost met last night."

To which Bob said, "Maybe I should have called first. Next time I will, promise."

"So . . . how did the game go?" she asked. We all answered at once, "We won!" perhaps louder than we should have. At which point, I looked down the road just to make certain there weren't any police cars headed our way.

"That's great! Congratulations! Does anyone want anything cold to drink?" Mike asked.

Bob replied, "Much appreciated, but it's late, and we better be getting back to campus." And with that, they got back into Joey's car and left. To my relief, no police ever showed up.

We walked up the steps and into our trailer, arms wrapped around each other. Mike looked at me and said, "It's nice to see a smile on your face, and I'm glad you came home safely. No incidents, no trouble." I looked back at her and, eager to change the subject, said, "Anything to eat?" I simply didn't want to tell her about the incident at the gas station.

No incidents, no trouble. Mike's words haunted me during the rest of the night. By morning, I had made my mind up. I had to tell her the truth. And if that was going to be her concern, I needed to nip it in the bud. She had allowed me to do so much, and I didn't want to add any more worry in her life. After all, I'd given my word that if there was any trouble, I'd stop playing.

I woke to the comforting smell of bacon, freshly fried and ready to eat. I hated to break the mood but couldn't hold it back. "I'm thinking about quitting the team," I yelled out from the bedroom. Mike came running down the hall, wooden spoon in hand.

"You're not going to hit me with that?" I said, looking at what was the makings of a pancake batter.

"What did you say? You're *what*?!" she said as she crossed the bedroom floor and stood over me, wooden spoon waving from side to side. She smelled a rat. "Okay, what are you not telling me?"

I told her about the Cambridge incident, but before I could get all the words out, her wooden spoon was perilously close to my face. "You're not quitting! Remember when we saw that team picture in the newspaper. Yeah, I'll admit, I was annoyed and scared for you. For us. But you made a commitment to Bob, to the team. And you said it was Bob who went to bat for you and got you on the team.

He's the one who's made you feel welcomed on campus. And you're quitting on him? No!"

"I know. I know," I said, trying to ease the tension. "It's eating at me. But things are really starting to get ugly out there on the Eastern Shore. Blacks are starting to protest. Whites are getting violent about it. And here I am riding straight through it on my way to play golf. Does that not sound crazy or what? I didn't realize it was this bad until I saw the faces of people riding past our car, looking at me . . . looking at them. If looks could kill, we would have been an easy target in that car."

"You know, I'm going to school for us. You know I love golf. And I'm really trying to recognize my own prejudices, which is a lot harder than I thought—but I also don't want to be a victim of hate, either. I need to be here for you, and wasn't it you who was originally afraid for my safety?"

"I've been reading the papers too, Fred," Mike said, suddenly stronger in voice though quieter in tone. "So you're not telling me anything I don't already know. But quitting is not the answer. We have lived with segregation all our lives. It's not going to disappear tomorrow, but we have to see it for what it is—hateful and mean. Your being the first white person to play on a Black college team may not change the world, but at least it will show the people who read that damn sports page that maybe it's time for a change. So go on, get your degree as we planned, play your golf games, make friends, and improve our immediate world. I think you're smart enough to make sure you don't take unnecessary chances. You're the one who opened my eyes, but you need to do what's right for us. The choice is yours, but it has to be something you believe is based in common sense, not fear."

As I headed toward English class the following day, Bob was standing at the door with a newspaper in hand. "Did they write about our win?" I asked, with a smile and a tap on his arm.

"Yup. We made the front page of the sports section of the *Salisbury Times*. Again."

Sure enough, there it was. The headline read: *Maryland State Duo lead golf team to trounce Morgan State!* Along with the article was a picture of Bob and me. My ego bounced back and forth between feeling good and feeling concerned. I shoved the concern aside. I didn't know what came over me, but for the first time, I got cocky. Maybe it was Mike's lecture, but at that point I didn't care what anyone thought about me being on an all-Black golf team, much less going to a Black college. I wasn't going to let those hateful assholes embarrass me, or the team, or the school.

After breakfast, I drove down to Pocomoke, found the nearest newsstand, and bought all the issues of the *Salisbury Times* that I could find. I then took off for the golf course.

I sat in the front seat of my old Ford, tearing out the front pages of all the Sports sections and with a pen circled Bob's and my picture on every one. I then wrote under the picture: "To the maintenance man. The above picture is the golfer on our team whom you called 'BOY.'" When the pro shop was empty, I taped all the pictures up on the wall.

When our golf team returned to the course for our next practice, the pro said he didn't know which one of us posted the newspaper articles on the wall, but the maintenance man saw them, tore them down, and stomped out. "We haven't seen him since. Guess he quit!"

Bob and I just stoically nodded our heads in unison, our faces blank, but knowing that the man had gotten what he deserved. As we walked out the door and headed to the driving range, we just looked at each other and smiled.

Our next match was in Washington, D.C., against Howard University, one of the most prominent Black universities in the country.

We were to play at Langston Golf Course, named for John Mercer Langston, an African American born free in the state of Virginia long before the Civil War. He went on to become a Virginia congressman and the dean of the College's Law School. I knew nothing about Howard University, John Mercer Langston, or much that related to what Blacks had to put up with to play the game of golf. It was Oscar who knew his history. I had asked him a few questions about the course and its history, and he was happy to clue me in about the importance of the place on our way to Washington.

"When Langston opened in 1939," Oscar said, "it was no better than the golf course we practice on. It had rutted greens and trash-strewn fairways, but it was better than nothing. Today, it's one beautiful course to play."

In the 1960s, Langston was playing host to African-American celebrities and was dubbed the "Home of Golf" for "Negroes." Originally built on top of a local dump, it opened with missing grass on the fairways and only nine holes. But the local players called it home. Over the years, the greens became green, garbage was removed, and it evolved into a respectable venue.

Once the history lesson was over, Oscar started talking about the difficult time it was for Black golfers to play the game. "Black golfers had started playing in the early 1800s, and we were good. The problem was trying to get on any golf course. Black players were only allowed on most public courses one day a week, and then they could only play in the afternoon when the sun was at its strongest. And there's no way in hell that we can get into any private clubs unless we caddy, cook, or serve. Fred, did you ever notice that before last year, the PGA didn't have any Black players? Now they only have one! Charlie Sifford, and it wasn't easy for him to get in! There's a reason."

"Geez, you're right," I said. "When I play golf, I just concentrate on my game. I never thought about it from a different point of view."

"Well, isn't that just like you whites! You don't think about it, 'cause you don't even see it. Let me tell you this: If you had seen me playing in front of you, I guarantee you would have noticed."

That comment threw me for a loop. He was right. How could the guys on my team have looked at me, and not thought that I was a part of their problem? My mind started to conjure up all kinds of thoughts and a question came to mind that I needed to get out. Taking a deep breath inward, I asked if anyone in the car resented me being on the team . . . or thought that I was a racist. It was something I had been thinking about since our first team meeting. I didn't have the guts to ask Bob during lunch or at practice, but after what Oscar had described, I just needed to know.

Eugene spoke up first. "I didn't like the idea of playing with a white guy at first. This was supposed to be our team, and you weren't one of us."

"And what changed your mind, Eugene?" Bob asked.

"I got to *know* Fred a little bit. I never had anything to do with anyone white before."

Joey piped up next: "I've known *lots* of white assholes. Fred isn't one of 'em. He wouldn't be in this car, if he were."

To which Bob chimed in, "Hell, maybe the boy is color-blind!" to which a few chuckles were heard coming from the back seat.

Oscar then said, "I think if more white folk mingled with more Black folk, we wouldn't have demonstrations, 'Whites Only' bathroom signs, or even segregated schools. Nah, Fred's no racist. If he were, I'd quit the team right now! It's like Eugene said, 'When you get to know someone, his skin color disappears.'"

Oscar then went on to tell us about a white kid who would cross the tracks into his neighborhood to go fishing. They became friends and fished together. One day they stopped into the gas station to use their bathroom. His white friend went inside to use the facilities, while Oscar had to go to an outhouse at the back of the building.

I figured Oscar would say how humiliating that was, but he said just the opposite. "You grow up expecting it," were his words.

I looked at Bob, sitting next to me in the front seat. His face was pensive, deep in thought, but few words came out of his mouth when he finally said, "I don't think you're a racist."

I asked him how he knew that, and he said, "Because we can tell who's a fuckin' racist and who isn't, right from the start. And you're not one of 'em. *That's* how I know."

Then, as if on cue, the car we were riding in was pulled over by a Maryland State Trooper. I was driving Joey's car, a system that we found worked for us, and we watched as the policeman got out of his car and walked toward ours, his shiny boots and neatly pressed cop shirt announcing his presence.

He approached the driver's side, and said, "Roll down your window."

I looked at him and said, "Officer, I wasn't speeding."

He bent forward, put his face closer to mine, and announced in a loud voice, "Boy, that's not why I pulled you over. What you doin' driving a car full of 'Negroes'? Going to a protest?"

"No, sir. We're heading for Langston golf course. We're the Maryland State College Golf Team."

"Maryland State's for 'coloreds.' You 'colored'?"

My mouth felt like a bag of cotton balls had moved in, but I knew I had to keep my cool and just answer politely if we were to avoid trouble.

"No, sir," I mumbled.

"Then these guys didn't kidnap you or anything? They're not holding you against your will, are they?"

"Sir, I'm the one driving. I say where the car goes."

I could see his face twitch, and knew I'd maybe taken it a step too far. I quickly added "sir" to the end of my sentence, and he seemed to relax—a bit.

"'Coloreds' don't play golf. Where're your bags?"

As I opened the car door, he stepped back, but not before putting his hand on the gun strapped to his waist. "The rest of you, put your hands up where I can see 'em and stay put," he growled as I moved slowly toward the back of the car, opened the trunk, and showed him the five golf bags stuffed into the trunk. Not quite satisfied that we were who we said we were, he then asked, "Who you playing this golf game with?"

"Howard University, sir, and if we don't move along, we'll be late for our match."

He nodded and watched as I walked back to my side of the car. He then looked straight at me and said, "Boy, what're you doin' at a 'colored' school? Couldn't get into any white colleges?"

I couldn't resist. "No, sir. This was the only school that would accept me." Not knowing if I was pulling his leg or not, he hesitated before shaking his head and spitting on the ground. With that he turned around and got into his car.

We all sat there until he pulled away. Then the laughter coming from inside the car could practically be heard all the way across town!

We pulled up the drive to Langston, found a parking spot, and untangled and unpacked our golf bags before finding Coach Briggs. He'd come up the night before and was staying at a friend's house. His face told us there was trouble brewing, and we all thought it was because we had given Morgan State a run for their money the previous week. Howard was trying to make life difficult for us. Looking at me, Coach said Howard's coach thought it was unfair for me to play with this team.

"Why? Because I'm white?"

"No. Because when you went to College Park and played varsity golf, you now play with an advantage."

"Wait, wait, wait," I interrupted the coach. "He thinks I played on the golf team? Nope! I did play varsity on a College Park team, but it was in wrestling. The last time I checked, the only wrestling you do in golf is in your own head!" By the time our coach returned with Howard's coaches' apology, we were ready to tee off.

The events of the day charged me up because I played my best round of the season. I shot a seventy-seven, our team won, and I guess their coach was pissed.

As it turned out, the Langston Golf Course wasn't too far from the National Mall in Washington, D.C. So once the game was over, and we had some free time anyway, we decided to walk to the Lincoln Memorial before we headed home. We approached the memorial and as we went up the stairs, we were quiet and respective. What I saw was beautiful. That feeling for love of country gave me goosebumps. Engraved above the statue were the words, "IN THIS TEMPLE AS IN THE HEARTS OF THE PEOPLE FOR WHOM HE SAVED THE UNION THE MEMORY OF ABRAHAM LINCOLN IS ENSHRINED FOREVER."

We left without saying a word to each other. As we neared the car, Oscar came over and said, "The North may have won the war, but too many of us still carry around shackles. You may not see them, but they are there." There was nothing I could say. Oscar had seen the same statue and read the same words I had, but he obviously had experienced the world in a vastly different way—one I was only just beginning to understand.

Our winning streak continued throughout the season, with Bob crushing drives down the middle of the fairways consistently. I had never seen anyone play golf as well as he did. As for me, Bob constantly tried to get under my skin. He'd say, "Engh, you're lazy! If you would quit being lazy, you could be a good golfer. Concentrate!" I knew he was right. What he was seeing was my inability to stand still. Where Bob could carefully focus on each shot, I tended to move around. It had been a problem all throughout my schooling, with teachers telling me to stop fidgeting, but I couldn't. With golf however, even with all the moving around, I played a good game. But to Bob's credit, he wanted me and the others on our team to play the best we could, and if trash talking was how he was going to do it, it seemed to be working.

In the weeks between matches, Bob and I would travel to Baltimore and play golf at different public courses that allowed Blacks to play with whites. Just the two of us. One day, a foursome of white guys who had teed off just before us was on the putting green for the first hole. Bob teed off on the 335-yard downhill hole. His ball flew toward the green where one guy in the foursome was just starting to putt. Bob's ball rolled past the green, and as it did, the golfers on the green all turned around to see who had hit the ball. They thought, surely the ball didn't come from us. We were too far away.

When we reached the next hole, the foursome was just approaching their green. Bob waited until they got onto the green then hit his ball. It landed ten feet in front of the green. I guess the players weren't too happy about our ball invading their territory. One of them started walking towards us, his arms flailing at his sides. There was no doubt that he was furious, and I knew he was going to give us an earful. So did Bob.

As he got closer, Bob came up and towered over me, and the angry fellow's head had to pitch higher and higher just to catch an eyeful of Bob. At twenty yards away, his pace slowed, and the steam coming out of his ears dissipated. After storming towards us for nearly 300 yards, then catching the size of Bob, the lion turned into a lamb and he meekly said to Bob, "Sir, would you mind waiting until we're off the green before you tee off?"

He quickly turned around and walked towards his green and teammates. I turned to Bob and said, "Well, at least he didn't call you 'boy'!"

That's the way it was between Bob and me. The color difference had morphed into one that we could joke about. We felt easy in each other's company. The more time we spent together, the more we learned about each other's lives.

It seemed like every Saturday morning I'd get my work done early around the house and get permission from the "boss" to play golf. Bob and I decided to play at the Elks club in Salisbury this one Saturday. I needed to finish our round early because I had a gig that night in Salisbury.

I told Bob that Chris, Dave, my brother Lynn and I were going to stop by Johnny's after our gig to play a few numbers. Chris and Dave had always wanted to meet Bob, having heard me talk about his ability to play football and golf.

When we finished our game, Bob dropped me off at the trailer and headed back to the campus. I told him we'd pack up and head to Johnny's around ten. The party we were booked for would finish early that night and I'd meet him there.

When all of us walked into Johnny's, we immediately found Bob sitting at the bar, a large Coca-Cola in front of him, and several attractive young ladies surrounding his chair. As soon as he saw us, he told the girls his friends had just come in and he needed to say hello. We found a table to sit at and ordered a pitcher of beer. Chris and Dave fawned over Bob. Lynn joined Bob's fan club as well. There was talk about Bob possibly going to the pros, but he played it down. He could have easily bragged about the scouts who were watching him, but he didn't. Bob wasn't like that. He was a gentle giant.

A few more pitchers of beer and Cokes were served, and the more we drank, the fuzzier I got in my head. I had forgotten to eat dinner, and the bowls of peanuts on the bar weren't enough to quell my appetite or curb my level of intoxication. When we got up to leave, Bob said he would drive me home. "I'm not letting you drive. Leave your car here. Tomorrow, we'll come back and pick it up." Since Lynn and the other guys lived in the other direction, it seemed like a good idea—especially since I probably couldn't find my car, anyway.

When we got to our trailer, Bob walked me to the door and gently knocked. He knew there were children asleep in the house and didn't want to wake them or scare Mike.

Bob told me later that the look on Mike's face was classic. She saw Big Bob and little Fred, as limp as a fish and leaning into Bob, and immediately knew what the situation was. "He's all yours," I kind of remember Bob saying to Mike. "Afraid he had too many pitchers of Budweiser. I didn't want him driving, so I'm leaving him on your doorstep."

I staggered into the trailer. Mike pointed me toward the bedroom, then invited Bob in to have a cup of coffee. "If Fred has had too many, maybe you need a coffee too to drive home," she said.

"No, ma'am. I don't drink alcohol. Coca-Cola's my guilty pleasure."

"Come in, anyway, and let me thank you with a Coca-Cola and a piece of cake."

I didn't know it that night, but Bob and Mike spent a lot of time just talking. When I made my way into the kitchen the next morning, I found Mike fiddling with the *Salisbury Times'* crossword puzzle. Without looking up from the paper, she asked, "You feeling better?"

"Like a cat that's been dragged home after a long night of prowling," was about all I could say. "I don't know how much I drank, but the pitchers of Bud just kept coming."

"That's what Bob told me. He came in, and we had a nice conversation while you passed out in the bedroom. And you were right . . . he is *a very nice person.*"

"What'd you talk about?" I asked.

"What life was like for him in the South. How his family had to endure the hardships of Jim Crow life in South Carolina, working in the fields, scrimping to put food on the table, raising kids—and how he turned out to be such a good friend . . . . by *not* letting you drive."

Bob also told Mike how athletics was so important to him or any Black kid. It was the only way they could break out of the poverty of segregation—the only way toward a better life.

"I think his mother had a lot to do with that. Apparently, she was the strength in the family. She reined all of them in. When they weren't in school, she borrowed books from the library and made them read."

"That's what a mother does, doesn't she?"

I looked at Mike, knowing she was the glue in our family. Without her holding us together, who knows where we would be.

"I love you, Mike."

"And I love you, Fred. But that doesn't excuse you from having to be carried into the house last night because of too many beers!"

"You're right," I said. "I almost forgot what a hangover was like, and it won't happen again . . . unless Bob's nearby."

With that, Mike playfully whacked me over the head with her crossword puzzle. *Ouch*!

1962 TIMELINE

January 3, 1962. After sixteen years in the House, Adam Clayton Powell became chairman of the Education and Labor Committee, the most powerful position held by an African American in Congress. As chairman, he supported the passage of important social and civil rights legislation under presidents John F. Kennedy and Lyndon B. Johnson. Powell was elected as a Democrat to represent the Congressional District that included Harlem. He was the first Black Congressman elected from New York State.

January 23, 1962. Jackie Robinson, the first African American to play Major League Baseball and winner of Rookie of the Year in 1947, was inducted into the Baseball Hall of Fame. His signing for the Brooklyn Dodgers in 1947 put an end to the color barrier in professional sports and heralded the end of racial segregation in Major League Baseball.

February 3, 1962. Several hundred "Freedom Riders" led by the NAACP carried out biracial sit-ins in the town of Chestertown, located in the Eastern Shore of Maryland. Most of the town's public facilities—schools, hospitals, theaters, restaurants, bowling alleys, and skating rinks—were still segregated. A large group of protesters faced off in a violent confrontation with white counter-protesters carrying makeshift weapons and baseball bats. State and local police broke up the altercations.

February 12, 1962. A bus boycott to end segregation and to open up employment to Black drivers and mechanics began in Macon, Georgia and lasted three weeks. Judge William

Bootle interceded and forced the desegregation of Macon's bus transportation.

March 10, 1962. Members of the Philadelphia Phillies baseball club, the last team to integrate in the National League, left the Jack Tar Harrison Hotel—their spring training base—due to the hotel's refusal to admit Black and Latino players to their restaurants and rooms.

August 15, 1962. Shady Grove Baptist Church in Leesburg, Georgia became one of four Black churches torched for being a base of SNCC activities. Civil Rights leaders, including Dr. Martin Luther King, spoke out against the two white men who were arrested and charged.

September 11, 1962. Thurgood Marshall, lawyer for the NAACP, after overcoming months of dissent among congressional members, was appointed judge of the 2nd Circuit Court of Appeals by President John F. Kennedy.

September 20, 1962. James H. Meredith, Jr., an African-American Air Force veteran, was denied admission to the University of Mississippi, known as "Ole Miss." Meredith attempted to register four times without success. He was only admitted after intervention by the U.S. Attorney General Robert F. Kennedy's sending federal marshals to accompany Meredith onto the campus. Rioting erupted, two people died, and dozens were injured. Meredith attended classes the following day, ending segregation at the University of Mississippi.

November 20, 1962. President Kennedy barred religious or racial discrimination in federally funded housing, a symbolic step toward addressing discriminatory housing and lending practices.

10

End of the Season

It wasn't easy for me to get out of the house to play a round of golf. Mike took care of everything there was to do when it came to caring for the kids, cleaning, cooking, and grocery shopping. She was now caring for two children under the age of two and an infant, born in February. I knew it was hard on her, especially when the spring weather started to turn humid, and we didn't have air conditioning. I had tried to do my share of caring for the kids and maintaining things around the outside of the trailer, not to mention studying and writing lesson plans for my part-time teaching job. But every once in a while, I really needed a break, but I also wanted to be fair to Mike. In talking to Bob, we came up with a plan.

I would get up early on Saturday mornings and start right in with the pruning, trimming, and watering the garden surrounding our trailer. I would then wash the windows on the outside. Once I had exhausted everything I could think of doing, including turning the hose onto the car, I would sheepishly approach Mike and asked if there was anything else she wanted me to do. Of course, she would say "No," and then I would ask if she minded if I played a few holes of golf. "Go on, Fred. You need a little downtime," she would say, and that's all the signal I needed. I would dial Bob, and tell him "Permission Granted." My clubs were already stashed in the trunk of the car, and a couple of bologna and mayonnaise sandwiches were stuffed in a bag.

It was like playing hooky, only my wife wouldn't rap me on the knuckles when I got home. Of course, being on a college golf team had its advantages. Many of the golf courses allowed team members to play for free. We made sure we booked time on those courses. And since gasoline was only thirty-cents a gallon, we were able to have an afternoon of golf for less than two dollars. The time we spent together also allowed us to talk about our lives. Over time stories got more personal and revealed a lot about who we were, and where we were heading.

I knew that while football wasn't Bob's first love, it was his way out of the South. He and his family called Columbia, South Carolina their home. He would refer to it as the "Deep South." It was a place of segregated schools, segregated neighborhoods, and segregated lives. For Bob, there were two different worlds living side by side; and the only times the Black people crossed over the line to the white neighborhoods was when it was time to cook, clean, or work for the white man. And when they were finished doing their jobs, they would head back across that line. His family history was packed with stories that made my skin crawl, but I never saw any rancor, anger, or hostility coming from him. When I asked him about it, his only response was: "What's getting mad going to do for me? Maybe land me in jail . . . or worse. Nah, man, I'll never change the white attitude toward us, so it's up to me to make my mark some other way."

And he did. He told me that, in 1960, he had been honored by the All-Central Intercollegiate Athletic Association (CIAA), the first historically Black collegiate athletic conference in football. Originally the "C" stood for "Colored" when the organization was founded in 1912, but was changed in 1950 to read "Central." Bob called that "progress."

There never was any doubt about our being friends. Our race and upbringing may have differed, but poor was poor whichever way you cut it. He laughed when I told him about our garage apartment in Ocean City and how all of us kids slept on mattresses on the floor. And I laughed when he told me how he crammed his big feet into his younger brother's smaller gym shoes just so he could skirmish with the high school team. But that was one of the joys of being friends. I learned about him, and he learned about me. And there we were, working our way through the golf courses of Maryland.

On the Saturday before Easter, I told Bob I had to go up to the University of Maryland's main campus in College Park and asked if he would like to drive along. "I'd love for us to play on the University course. I'm not sure we can get a tee time, but if we get there early enough, maybe they can fit us in." I managed to get all my work done before the crack of dawn. By 7:00 A.M., we were on the road.

The University's main campus is what every college should look like. Red brick buildings covered in ivy, with white columns soaring several stories up, a central quad filled with students lazing in the sun and surrounded by other Georgian buildings. At the top end of the quad was the stately McKeldin library where the bronze Maryland terrapin mascot, "Testudo," a gift from the class of 1933, held forth in front, waiting for his nose to be rubbed for good luck. It was the epitome of what a college campus should look like.

But what impressed me the most were the students. Black, white, orange, brown—all walked together as one unit. So different from the Maryland State Campus. Bob told me that only a few years back, the Supreme Court of the United States removed any legal basis for segregation at the University of Maryland, opening up the campus to all. There were still segregated sororities and fraternities lining the horseshoe-shaped fraternity row across the street from the Quad, and the protests were still relatively minor, but Maryland was as close to an Ivy League school as you could get at that time, without the price tag.

The golf course was tucked into the rolling hills west of the campus. We started out at the driving range, needing a bit of warm-up after the long drive. I told Bob I would go into the clubhouse and see if we could get a tee time. As I opened the door, an old friend of mine from one of my University of Maryland physical education classes was coming out. He had been on the University's golf team and was one of the best. When I went to the campus, he and I would talk incessantly about golf in our different physical education classes. I was sure I drove him crazy. He had graduated but lived close enough to play whenever he could.

We had chatted for just a few minutes when he asked me if I wanted to play with him and his friend, another former golf team member. They needed players to round out their foursome. "Great," I told him. "I came with a friend of mine. Do you mind if he joins us? He's a great golfer."

"Not a problem," he said. "We'll meet you at the first tee."

I went back to the range and said to Bob, "Man, we got lucky. We're going to play with a couple guys who were on the Maryland golf team. How's that for luck?"

As we approached the first tee, my friend spotted us. He first waved at me with a big grin; one that disappeared, though, when he saw Bob walking next to me. It jolted me. I saw him whisper something to his golf partner and watched as both turned around again and eyed Bob. I knew what was coming.

In the meantime, Bob, who seemed to already know what was going, said, "Why don't you meet me back at the range." He apparently decided to let me handle things myself.

The closer I got, the more pissed I became thinking that my so-called friend didn't want to be seen playing golf with some Black guy. As soon as I got there, he started to grill me about me not telling him about my "friend," as though he were afraid to say the words "Black man."

It would have been easy for me to call him and his friend racist jerks, but I tried to keep my cool. I told him that he had never given me any warning about his being afraid to play against Black people.

"As it turns out," I said, "Bob and I are on the Maryland State College golf team, and we're slated to win the conference championship."

"You go to Maryland State?" he asked incredulously.

"Sure do. What do you say to that?"

"Only 'coloreds' go there."

"Only 'coloreds'—and *me*," I shot back at him, inching closer to his face.

"Man, I didn't take you for one of them. I guess you're one of those kinds who rides the freedom bus."

It took all the strength I had to not punch him in the face, but enough was enough. "All this time," I began, "and I had no idea that you were a fucking racist. You think you and your friend here are better than them? Well, I would rather be one of them than either of you. And your time for putting down anyone who doesn't look like you is coming to an end! Get over it, because the world is changing!" Having said my peace, I then simply walked away.

When I reached the range, I knew Bob was pissed. We never did play a round of golf that day. On the way to the car, he said to me, "Engh, I'm proud of you."

Growing up, I had a lot of friends. Drinking buddies, beach buddies, Army buddies. But after I got married and had responsibilities, those friends dropped off the radar. And as I learned the hard way, going to an all-Black school didn't help either. I involved myself with work so we had a place to live and enough to eat, and spent time being a Dad to my kids. At that point in my life, I can honestly say that outside of my siblings, Bob was one of my only friends. I talked to him about everything, sharing my worries and goals; most of the time, race didn't even enter into the conversation for us. Maybe it should have come up, but I no longer saw him as a Black man, the way I did that first day on campus. All I saw was someone who I could talk to, laugh with, and depend upon to have my back. Unfortunately, it seemed it was always white people who would remind me that Bob was Black.

I had reached a point in my mind where I knew where I was going. I was on my way to getting a teaching certificate, and the working world was just ahead. I had a real career in front of me. Mike was happy to see me on track, and for the first time, my grades showed my commitment.

The apprehension I felt initially about going to Maryland State had disappeared. I was now just another student. As I sat in the Student Union, waiting for my next class, I found myself sitting with five other Black students. We first started talking about sports. They all apparently knew that I was on the golf team, and we talked about how well we were playing. Surprisingly, the subject turned to Black and white relationships. I was asked how I felt going to an all-Black school. I told them that I was impressed when, from the start, the students there had all treated me fairly—not at all like someone who was invading their turf.

"How has your experience being on a Black campus changed you . . . a white man?" someone asked. For the first time since being at Maryland State, I was being asked by Blacks to describe what it meant to be white on their campus. It was all an epiphany for me. These Black students were not shy about talking about race. We were all equal, and they were treating me as one of their own. They all stopped talking and looked at me, waiting for an answer. I tried to look pensive, and said slowly, "I'm *white*?"

At first, they didn't quite know how to respond, but one by one they all started to laugh. I began to laugh as well. It was a good way to break the ice, but from there I got serious.

"How has being in this school changed me, huh? Well, for one thing, it's opened my eyes to what segregation really is and how it's affected not only Black people but whites as well. Imagine how advanced our country would be if we were all color-blind? If Blacks had the same advantages as whites?"

One of the students sitting nearby joined in: "But that's not gonna happen, not in my lifetime."

I countered him. "Only if you accept segregation. But by being here, you're already putting yourself ahead of the game. Don't give up or give in. Learn how to operate in a white man's world, while introducing them to the Black man's world, and before you know it, you'll be the one they're opening the doors to."

"Just like you've learned to operate in a Black man's world?"

"Yeah. I was nervous at first. Felt out of place. I didn't expect everyone on campus to like me or want to be my friend but was happy that so many of you went out of your way to just say 'hello' when we passed in the hall."

"And then there's my own personal prejudice," I continued. "I grew up with my own parents keeping their distance from Black people. Whether it was business or social things, Blacks were always excluded. They never called Black people names, but that was no excuse for the way they behaved. And while I may not have known it growing up, that uneasiness about being around anyone Black was there. It wasn't that I was afraid as much as it was needing to stick to our own. And it was only until I came here that I saw it for what it was."

I couldn't believe I was actually telling these people what I had been thinking about all those past months. I started out wanting to get a diploma, but my education was expanding into areas I had never really thought about. The person I used to be was not the person who sat in that Student Union speaking comfortably about segregation and its effect on my life.

After I finished, one of the guys said, "Maybe you're not as white as you think you are."

As we played through our season, I guess the other teams realized that Bob was the reason behind our winning streak. Nobody ever questioned me about playing on a varsity team at College Park again, and no one mentioned that a white guy was wearing the Maryland State Hawks golf shirt. Sit-ins continued, but most were low-key and didn't involve violence. That would come later. I grew very comfortable being a white person in a Black person's world, especially on the golf course.

We slammed our competition and by the end of spring, we had won our championship. After all the hullabaloo was over about our winning the championship, after holding the Championship Cup in our hands and posing for pictures, including for the *Salisbury Times*, Coach McCain called Coach Briggs and the team into his office.

While we were celebrating our season, Coach Briggs was told by the college administrators that because of budget cuts, golf was being dropped from the athletic budget. There would be no golf team next season. We were saddened, but not surprised as Coach had warned us at the beginning of the season. Even though we had brought honor to the school and were winners, they were canning us, and the golf program. We discussed paying for our own expenses to play, but that idea fell through when the coach told us how much we would need. We realized we didn't have the money it would take to continue. Our winning season became our *last* season.

When the final class for the semester was over, Bob and I said our good-byes for the summer. He left for his home in Columbia, South Carolina to spend a summer picking up odd jobs and getting ready for his last year of college football. I was desperate to find a job to tide us over until school started at St. Francis, since they only paid me during the school year.

"Lady Luck" was on my side when my brother, Lynn, called to say that our band had been invited to play at the new Carousel Hotel in Ocean City. It was opening in July and little did we know that the majority owner was a big political contributor. Busses of champagne-fueled Congressional members would arrive at the hotel, ready to party. The word spread quickly that the Carousel was the place to be, drawing celebrities and even more politicians. It was to become the local hot spot, and we would be in the middle of it, playing six nights a week. For me, it meant a nice paycheck and lots of driving.

Mike and I decided that it would be best to pack up the trailer and move it to a place in Ocean City. It just made sense as I got my old job back renting beach umbrellas during the day and I was playing in the band now six nights a week—into the wee hours of the morning. Plus, Muzzie was close by in Ocean City to help Mike with our growing family. The only downside was that I was a lot farther away from the Maryland State Campus, but the financial stability I had was worth the extra commuting time.

Summer turned into fall, and I was back in school. This would be my last year and in just ten months I would have my Physical Education degree, if the world didn't fall apart first.

Rumblings of racial discord continued in Cambridge, Maryland, which wasn't surprising considering how our golf team was greeted when we stopped for gas the previous spring. The sit-ins and freedom rides were growing in numbers and the Cambridge Nonviolent Coordinating Committee, an affiliate of the Student Non-Violent Coordinating Committee, started picketing businesses that refused to hire Blacks, and that included local governmental defense contractors. Unfortunately, these protests were often disrupted by gangs of whites, and they often became violent.

Our campus remained fairly quiet during those turbulent times, but we could feel the tension. And then October 16, 1962 happened. For thirteen days, the campus, our country, and the rest of the world looked as if we were headed toward a nuclear war. The

United States and the Soviet Union were at odds when the U.S. discovered nuclear missile sites being built in Cuba. Everyone would go to class as usual, but every day the news seemed to be getting worse. We talked about whether we should study for tests or not. No matter where you were, the conversations about the protests in Cambridge took second place to talk about whether or not there would be a nuclear holocaust, and if there could really be any winners. It didn't seem to matter what color your skin was—atomic bombs played no favorites—and throughout the next two weeks, everyone held their collective breaths. And as quickly as it started, it ended with each side agreeing there would likely be no winners in any confrontation.

I hadn't run into Bob in Registration, in the school cafeteria, or on campus until late October. His football practice schedule and courses were not in sync with mine as they were the previous year. As I was crossing the parking lot heading to a class, I spotted him and called out his name, waving to catch his attention. Unlike before, there was no smile when we were face to face—only silence. Then he said, "What the hell's with you, man? I called you when I got back so we could play golf. No answer. Phone disconnected. I go to your trailer. It's gone. I'm beginning to believe all that shit you told me about being friends was a joke. I'm thinking you been using me for the last year. I have a phone. Why the fuck haven't you called me?"

I stood there, stunned. I'd never seen this side of Bob before, his anger, and now it was directed at me. And he wasn't wrong. I was pulled in so many directions over the summer that staying in touch with him had just slipped past me.

Words didn't come easily, but I finally got it together and said, "You're right. I am an ass, but since I last saw you, my life has spun around. I had to pack and move the trailer back to Ocean City. The band is playing six nights a week and I've just been going crazy shuffling between two jobs, my home life, playing until early morning with the band, and commuting. And I had to organize my classes to be sure I had all my credits before I spend next semester student teaching."

"So that just leaves me out of the picture, huh?" Bob continued, still upset.

I was humiliated by Bob's words, knowing that I was close to losing a good friend. And worst of all, I knew he was right. The only thing I could tell him was the truth. "I'm sorry about not telling you that we moved, but I didn't have your number in South Carolina. Over the summer, I got an opportunity to make some decent money playing with Lynn's band in Ocean City. We moved the trailer there so my mother could help Mike with the kids and to make my commute easier. I should have reached out to you when classes began, but being the idiot I am, I didn't."

Bob looked at me as a soft smile crossed his face. "Well, I guess you're good for one more chance, white boy." And he punched me in the arm, just like old times. "So, when are we playing golf? Saturday?"

"I can't. I have to officiate at a soccer game. It's part of my 'Officiating' class."

"Just playing with you, Fred" he said. "I've got a football game to play that day, anyway. Look . . . I'll give you my new number, and you give me yours . . . just make sure you call me for a game before the snow falls, okay?"

While we occasionally ran into one another on campus, between Bob's football schedule and my own priorities, we never did get to play another game of golf together.

11
Officiating

I woke up early that Saturday morning, ready to officiate at the soccer match. Officiating was one of my last required classes, probably an "easy A, and a four-credit 'A'" at that. As long as I did what I was supposed to do, there was little chance of screwing up that grade. At least, that's what I thought when I was getting ready to go to the game. What I didn't realize was that in officiating, the difference between an "A" and an "F" might be a lot closer than I could ever have imagined.

"Pop" Watson, the Physical Education department head, also taught the Officiating class and while we had gone over all the rules and regulations of many games in class, the prospect of actually officiating on the field was intimidating. Pop assigned five of us to referee the soccer match at a local high school; and because I was never really a soccer player, I made sure to refresh myself on the rules of the game the night before. Our performance on the field was going to be an important part of our grade.

"Pop" hired a van to take us to the high school, and on the way over discussed all we needed to pay special attention to while officiating. He was a low-key kind of guy and slipped in the fact that the game was being played between two Black high schools, both of which were tied going into the championship season. And there I was, the only white guy, the sacrificial lamb when a bad call was made. I started to sweat.

As we walked onto the field, I noticed the bleachers were filled with parents and fans from both schools, and I felt that all eyes were staring at me. Once again, that image of Muzzie's matchsticks popped into my head, and I started to tense up. Being on an all-Black campus was one thing. Being in front of hundreds of people who only saw me for the color of my skin was another. All I could imagine them thinking was what the hell was a white guy doing judging their children.

Still, I was one of the officials and I had to concentrate on what I needed to do. That meant that I would be one of the men who would be determining who would win and who would lose. Whatever call we gave, it would be wrong, depending on what side you were on. The only thing going for us was that both teams were from Black schools and had obviously played well enough to get to the top of the standings. I don't want to think about what would have happened if one of the teams was from a white school.

The stands erupted when the players came onto the field, and when the starting whistle rang out, loud war cries seemed to echo from the stands. The thing about reading the rules and understanding how to apply them to a game quickly became evident. I didn't want to make a wrong call knowing it might cause some contention among the impassioned fans. So then and there I decided to just run up and down the field, looking official, and like I knew what I was doing. That might have worked anywhere else, but my lack of officiating skill was apparent to fans on both sides. Some began yelling a few choice words, raging about the white guy on the field—how did he get there, and why was he one of the refs? I thought to myself, *Hey, maybe I should be making some calls.* It was easy enough to see if a player stepped off the field or tripped another player intentionally. It didn't matter. They booed at any call I made, yelled profanities when I didn't react to a play, and basically made me feel like crap for the first half of the game.

When the halftime buzzer sounded, Pop sent the other referees to their locker room, pulled me aside and gave me two minutes of his best. "Look, Fred, being a game official at any event like this will always have people who are going to yell something at you whatever your call. But this game is different. The district championship is ahead of both teams, and a white guy is calling plays that may or may not change the outcome of the game. Your calls aren't wrong. Your color is. And you're getting a good taste of what it's like being a minority."

I stood on the sidelines for the rest of the game, and as Pop suggested, I held a clipboard in my hand and tried to look as if I was doing something relevant to the game, which I wasn't. When the game ended, all I can remember is that one of the teams won. As soon as the match was over, I ran for cover into the locker room.

I was nervous when I got to my Officiating course, my last class of the semester. It was only weeks away from the end of the semester and after what had happened to me at that soccer game, I wasn't sure what grade I was going to get. At the end of the class, Watson handed out folders to all the students with their evaluation and their final grade in it. He called out my name, and I went up to get my folder. I swallowed hard, slowly opened the folder, and was shocked. There, in big bold letters, was an "A," and alongside it, this explanation from the coach: "I apologize for what I said to you on the field when you officiated. You took a lot of heat, didn't fold, and for that I commend you. You deserve the 'A,' and I'm proud to give it to you."

That course gave me the four in-class credits I needed to graduate. Only a semester of student teaching was left. But that course taught me more than just officiating. The names I was being called at the game absolutely shook me up; but later, when I thought about it, I probably had no right feeling bad, considering what each and every person there had to go through every day of their lives. The thing of it was that the coach had the decency to reflect on his words and to empathize with what I was going through. Sometimes experience teaches you more about life than any textbook can.

1963 TIMELINE

January 14, 1963. George C. Wallace was sworn in as Governor of Alabama with a pledge of "segregation now, segregation tomorrow, segregation forever," a speech written by Ku Klux Klan leader Asa Carter. Known as the "speech that will live in infamy," his words defined white segregationist defiance against equal rights for Blacks.

February 15, 1963. The Northwood Theater, located in Baltimore, MD, refused to sell tickets to Black moviegoers. In an effort to raise public awareness, twenty-six Black students from Morgan State College entered the theater to purchase tickets. After being denied admission, they refused to leave. All the students were arrested, and released the next day.

April 2, 1963. Police reported that the Children's Crusade in Birmingham, Alabama—a non-violent demonstration led by Reverend Dr. Martin Luther King—began with police led by Eugene "Bull" Connor, bombarding the protesters and the children with high-pressure water jets and police dogs. As a result, Connor lost his job, all "Jim Crow" signs were removed, and public places were opened to all races.

June 11, 1963. The "Stand in the Schoolhouse Door" protest took place at Foster Auditorium at the University of Alabama. George Wallace, the Governor of Alabama, in a symbolic attempt to keep his inaugural promise of "segregation now, segregation tomorrow, segregation forever" and stop the desegregation of schools, stood at the door of the auditorium to try to block the entry of two African-American students, Vivian Malone and James Hood.

June 12, 1963. Medgar Evers, field director of the NAACP in Mississippi, was fatally shot in front of his home in Jackson by the Ku Klux Klan. An informant in the Klan, Delmar Dennis later served as a key prosecution witness in convicting Byron De La Beckwith for the slaying. Beckwith was convicted of murdering Evers and sentenced to life in prison.

August 28, 1963. The civil rights "March on Washington" for Jobs and Freedom was held, drawing over 250,000 demonstrators. It was the occasion for Dr. Martin Luther King to deliver his "I Have a Dream" speech given in front of the Lincoln Memorial, in which he called for an end to racism.

September 15, 1963. The Ku Klux Klan bombed the 16th St. Baptist Church in Birmingham, Alabama. Four young Black girls—Denise McNair, Carole Robertson, Addie Collins, and Cynthia Wesley—were killed in the bombing as they prepared their Sunday school lesson on "The love that forgives."

October 22, 1963. 225,000 students boycotted Chicago schools in a Freedom Day protest railing against "redlining" the city's school districts, overcrowding, and run-down facilities. While the protest didn't yield immediate results, it turned the city's attention to the crises.

November 22, 1963. John F. Kennedy, the 35th president of the United States was shot at 12:30 P.M. as his open limousine traveled through Dealey Plaza past the Texas School Book Depository. Within the hour, Kennedy was pronounced dead at Parkland Hospital.

12
Graduation Day

It was graduation day. A little less than two years ago I had walked onto the campus of Maryland State College—nervous, frightened, but determined to do what I had to do to get my degree and become a high school physical education teacher. I thought back to when I first approached the campus, reading the sign at the bottom of the big hill, looking up at all the Georgian brick and ivy, and watching all the nervous students as they registered, myself included. And on this sunny Saturday afternoon, the atmosphere was totally different. What I was seeing were beautifully dressed men and women, some with hats, some with flowers alongside their children, who were no longer children, dressed in caps and gowns heading up that hill, on their way to the auditorium where the ceremony would take place.

The graduating seniors lined up in the hallway outside the auditorium while Moms and Dads, grandparents, brothers, sisters, and nieces and nephews seated themselves in the audience. Soon we would march into the room to the traditional tune of Elgar's "Pomp and Circumstance." For all of us, graduating from college was an achievement that had been hard fought for. For many in the audience, a college education may have seemed like a dream. But for this graduating class, it was about to become a reality. It was an important step forward. An achievement we all hoped would allow us to build better lives for ourselves.

As I marched into the room, I spotted my wife, Mike, in the audience. She was all decked out in her Sunday best and pregnant with our fourth child—due in less than two months. As it turned out, Mike and I were not the only whites in attendance. There was one other. He was Senator Wayne Morse of Oregon. Why he was chosen to speak at our graduation ceremony remained a mystery to me, but his being the only U.S. Senator at that time opposed to the Vietnam War may have had something to do with it. It was also during the time of increasing racial tension. Maybe he was there to appraise the temperament of the student body. What I do know is that his eyes scanned the lineup of graduates and landed on me, and then he found Mike. His quizzical look was comic.

Mike may have had some apprehension about attending but understood what this day meant to me—and to our family. Muzzie offered to take care of the kids so Mike could attend and said she would see us afterward at her house for a celebration with the family. Sitting there in a sea of black faces, Mike finally got to experience what it was like to feel different because of the color of one's skin. As she sat there all alone, the man sitting next to her leaned over and said, "I think that's your husband down there in the front row, isn't it?"

"Is it that obvious?" she responded.

To which he replied, "Yes, ma'am, I'm afraid it is," and they both laughed.

After Senator Morse's speech, the President of Maryland State College, Dr. John T. Williams, gave his commentary on the pride he felt in our graduating class, the progress the school had achieved, especially in sports, and he could not refrain from mentioning the changing color of the student body. And with that, he started calling out the names of those getting degrees that day.

Mike was beaming as I made my way toward the front of the line when Dr. Williams called my name. My eyes scanned the audience and saw Mike standing and cheering, and then, his head popping up higher than the rest of the students, I saw Bob, a huge smile etched across his face. He was clapping along with the rest of them. We were both on our way to the rest of our lives.

Walking out the door of the auditorium was exhilarating. It was over. I had done it. I was on my way to a future that had promise. I thought about Bob and the amazing life he had in front of him, one that was likely to bring him success and the means to contribute to the family he had left behind in South Carolina. I wondered how many of the other graduates had an idea of what they were going to do with their lives.

As we drove over the dusty two-lane backroads toward Ocean City—the same roads on which I had driven so many times that last year of school—I was looking forward to this being the last time. I had my Physical Education degree. I had my teaching credentials, and a few real job offers were already in the pipeline. Maybe soon we could dump the trailer and move into a decent-sized apartment and trade-in my old Ford for a newer model. I was excited to show Muzzie the diploma that Mike so proudly held in her hands. Mike and I laughed about how she felt sitting in an auditorium and being the only white person in the room. She told me about the comment the man next to her made about her being my wife.

On our way to Muzzie and Coolie's, we passed a number of welcoming rural towns. I thought about the great memories I had when I was living in Ocean City, working on the beach during the day and enjoying what the town had to offer at night. I slowed down as we passed the Humane Society house. It was still standing, with a "FOR SALE" sign planted in the overgrown grass. I thought of Thelma and Josh, and wondered if Josh was still selling eggs, or had had the good fortune to attend college. Then something else struck me as I remembered those white kids harassing us because of his color. Small towns weren't as welcoming as they may have seemed. They were only welcoming to those of my color. If any of those students in my graduating class or their guests showed up there when I was a kid, it would have been a different story. And that would have probably never been a thought in my head had I not attended the college I did.

I was well aware that Americans were beginning to come to the realization that segregation and racial hate was built into the very fabric of our country. With sit-ins, marches, protesters, and freedom riders making the news every day, it was hard to miss. The problem may have been easy to spot in the Southern states under the Jim Crow laws that had legalized discrimination, but it was everywhere. I had grown up with it in Maryland.

Dr. Martin Luther King, Jr. had spoken about our country's need to change as a nation. And while he talked about the unfair practices that suppressed Blacks who tried to live a more decent and manageable American life, he also unveiled how deeply ingrained racism still was in our white culture less than a century after the Civil War and the "end" of slavery. Perhaps we could change the laws, but it was not likely that we could change the attitudes of those folks like that maintenance worker at the golf course, or that group of rednecks at the gas station, or the person we were going to celebrate my graduation with . . . Muzzie. If it weren't for my two years at Maryland State, I would likely have been one of those other white people—but I had changed.

Unfortunately, I thought to myself as I neared my destination, there was probably nothing anyone could do to change the generation that grew up seeing segregation as normal. But Mike and I had the opportunity to break the cycle with our own children, and at least that would be a good start.

We pulled into Muzzie's driveway. There, in the front of the house, were colorful signs celebrating my graduation. The front door opened, and Muzzie walked right up to me and put her arms around me. As she held me tight, she whispered, "I'm so proud of you, Freddy. I'm more than proud. I knew you could do it!"

"Muzzie, I want to tell you something," I said, as I held her at arm's length and looked into her eyes. "First, if it wasn't for you kicking me in the butt, this never would have happened. You were right. I was lost and didn't even know it. I think I have the future in front of me that you hoped I would have. And while I know you questioned me about going to Maryland State, if it weren't for the help those teachers gave me, I'm not sure if I could have made it through. And lastly, I think . . . hope . . . that what I learned will help make me a good teacher, but I think I learned a lot more than I was ever expecting to while I was there. And while I don't expect you to feel the way I do about some people, I hope I can teach my children some of the things I learned at Maryland State . . . and it's all due to you. Thank you."

I then said, "Muzzie, I have a gift for you."

"You have a gift for me? Are you kidding? *You're* the one who just graduated!"

"Muzzie, close your eyes and hold out your hand."

She looked at me like I was crazy, but she did it. Once her eyes were closed, I reached into my pocket and pulled out the item I had been holding all day long. I placed it into her palm, and said, "You can open your eyes." She looked at me, and then at the item I had placed in her hand. It was the book of matches that she had given me almost two years ago.

I said, "It's funny how much you can learn from matches . . . now, let's go in and eat. I'm starving!"

2012 TIMELINE

January 31, 2012. President Barack Obama declared February to be African-American History Month, and the celebration of Black Women in American Culture and History to be the theme of the first month of celebration.

February 22, 2012. President Obama and others took part in the formal groundbreaking for the National Museum of African-American History and Culture as part of the Smithsonian Institution museums located on the National Mall. The museum later formally opened on September 24, 2016.

February 26, 2012. In Sanford, Florida, Trayvon Martin—a seventeen-year-old African-American high school student—was fatally shot by George Zimmerman, a watch coordinator in the neighborhood where Martin was visiting his relatives. Martin was unarmed and taking a break from watching an NBA All-Star Game to walk to a convenience store to buy snacks. Initially, Zimmerman claimed self-defense under Florida's "Stand Your Ground" law. He was later charged with murder under the Federal Civil Rights Act, but was subsequently acquitted.

April 26, 2012. The Jim Crow Museum of Racist Memorabilia held its grand opening at Ferris State University in Big Rapids, Michigan. David Pilgrim, the founder and curator, started building the collection as a teenager. The museum houses a collection of over 10,000 items that reflect the various public images of racism between the 1870s and the 1960s.

June 20, 2012. Organized by the NAACP, tens of thousands of New Yorkers marched in silent protest against the city's "Stop and Frisk" policy, a practice that allows police to stop individuals if they suspect the person is committing a crime or preparing to do so. Protesters believe it is unfairly used against young Blacks and Hispanics.

September 27, 2012. In a poll conducted by the *Associated Press* as President Obama ran for his second term in office, researchers found that more Americans had attitudes that were both implicit and explicitly racist than when the same survey was conducted four years ago. In all, 51 percent of Americans now expressed explicit anti-Black attitudes, compared with 48 percent four years prior, the study showed. When measured by an implicit racial attitudes test, the number of Americans with anti-Black sentiments jumped to 56 percent, up from 49 percent during the last presidential election. In spite of these findings, Obama won the 2012 election.

October 16, 2012. A month before the Obama-Romney election, Donald Trump—in an effort to once again promote his Birther Conspiracy theory, a theory claiming that Obama was born in Kenya—offered to donate five million dollars to charity in return for the publication of Obama's college and passport applications before October 31, 2012. He did this in spite of Obama having released his birth certificate on April 27, 2011.

December 26, 2012. President Obama signed an executive order to establish the White House Initiative on Educational Excellence for African Americans, The initiative for African Americans was created so that every Black child has "greater access to a complete and competitive education from the time they're born all through the time they get a career."

13
The Hall of Fame

So much had happened to me in those years since graduation day so many years ago. But that's the truth of everyone who travels a life-journey filled with experiences. Without realizing how many years had actually passed, I found myself back at Maryland State College, now renamed The University of Maryland Eastern Shore. That was a name I had to keep repeating to myself over and over again, as it marked not only the transition of the College from an all-Black student body, to one that offered all who wanted an education the possibility, just as it did me back in the early 1960s. I was the only white student then. Now, in 2012, the campus was thoroughly integrated—as it should be.

Sitting there on the dais that night during the Hall of Fame presentations, I pinched myself more than once, thinking, *Being in the right place at the right time couldn't have been more appropriate.* I knew why I was here, but forty-nine years and a lot of life had come in between, and I had to actually sit back and reflect on how I had gotten to be one of the honored guests.

I had been featured in a story that The Golf Channel had aired about my going to an all-Black college and being the only white person on the golf team. I didn't think that many people saw the piece as my phone was not exactly ringing off the hook with congratulatory messages. But one person actually did see it—Keith Davidson, the athletic director at the University of Maryland Eastern Shore. He had called and said, "Our college's nominating committee has met and selected you to be a member of the school's Hall of Fame!"

They thought I was worthy because of my willingness to break the color barrier by attending the school and for being the first white member of the golf team—a team that had won the division title, no less. *How ironic*, I thought at the time. While Blacks were facing hostile groups of whites as they fought for the right to attend racially segregated schools, I simply walked into this school and registered. And beyond getting a degree, I made a good friend and got to play golf with him, for free. And yet, here I was, on the dais, being inducted for something that truly changed the course of my life.

I sheepishly stole a glance around the dais to see the other inductees, and I gasped as NFL Hall of Fame legend Art Shell (the former coach of the Oakland Raiders) stood signing autographs for well-wishers. Next to me was a vacant seat. The athletic committee had decided to leave the chair empty, with just a sign marking his name tacked to the front for all to see. It was to be for Clarence Clemons, a standout on the school's highly touted football team who went on to become the sax player in Bruce Springsteen's E-Street Band. He had accepted the school's invitation but had unfortunately died several months before the event. His name was on the chair "In Absentia."

I listened to a few of the speeches and, before I realized it, was being tapped to speak next. I learned that Bob had been inducted years before, but I never knew about his ceremony, and wished that he had been here at mine.

While I had spoken in front of people so much of my life, I suddenly became nervous, and my lengthy speech that I had practiced at home so many times was reduced to just a few sentences. After presenting me with a maroon jacket with the school's insignia emblazoned on the pocket, I mentioned Bob several times in my speech, told one or two stories about being the only white guy on the golf team, and finished by saying that getting my degree from this great school was a great honor.

Bob was clearly on my mind as I sat back down, and my thoughts drifted to some of the adventures we had as well as some of the pranks he had pulled on me and some I had pulled on him. My reverie was broken by the house lights coming up and the audience clapping. Everyone on the dais was standing up, smiling, shaking hands, and I was late to join in, my mind still on Bob and our friendship. A friendship that had been—and then wasn't.

On the way home, Mike noticed how quiet I was and asked what I was thinking. I told her that I had to find Bob.

"You're talking about Bob Taylor, aren't you?" she asked.

"Yep. That Bob. Being back at school, remembering how important he was to my getting through that first year, how could I have been so thoughtless and not have reached out?" The regrets flooded my mind—my never telling him how the priest at St. Francis who had helped me coach the rag-tag football team when we were in college had recommended me for the head football coaching job at St. Elizabeth High School in Wilmington, Delaware. I never heard that indefinable laugh when I told him that, in my first year of coaching, we tied for the conference championship. Would he have known how proud I was that he was drafted by the New York Giants and then played for the Minnesota Vikings? Damnit, I never congratulated him for kicking all the other NFL players' asses by winning the NFL pre-season golf tournament.

Friendships are funny things. To be meaningful you have to be able to pick up the phone and continue a conversation you left off years before. You need to be able to finish each other's sentences. You need to stand up for each other, laugh and cry with each other, have disagreements and then feel the punch in your arm when all is forgiven.

I was ashamed. I regretted not staying in touch with my friend. It had been forty-nine years since I saw Bob's big head popping up from the crowd of graduates and applauding me. "I've got to call him," I said to Mike. "I have to find him." I wanted one more time to hear the voice of the person who made it possible for me to look racism in the eye and say, "No more." I wanted to thank him for the opportunity he gave me to see his world.

We got home and I went straight to my desk. The one where my graduation diploma from Maryland State College still hung, above it on the wall. The drawers were jam-packed with papers, clips, pencils and pens, but what I was looking for didn't appear to be there. I dug deeper into the back and finally found what I was looking for—a letter I received from Bob a few weeks after graduation. The paper was old and the ink fading, but the words were still strong:

Dear Fred,

Sorry we never got to talk at graduation. I just wanted you to know how much I enjoyed our friendship. When I saw you at registration, you weren't hard to miss. You looked like a scared puppy. And when you ran into the police guard outside, I thought, "I got to help him before he gets himself thrown in jail." Growing up, I really never had a white friend. Remember when I called you "white boy?" I didn't think we would become friends. And it turned out that we did.

We did have some fun. The golf games. Playing jokes on each other. Just driving along, talking.

I don't think I ever told you, but your wife was the first white lady who ever invited me into her home past the kitchen. That is something I will never forget. I saw her in the audience and couldn't help noticing that she's having another baby. After this one, give her a break! No more kids!

I wish you could have met my Mama. She'd have loved you. I wish you success in whatever you do, and I look forward to hearing about your getting a hole in one, but not until you hear about mine!

Bob Taylor

I read Bob's letter over and over again, its words digging a hole in my heart.

The following Monday, I was up early and turned on my computer. The internet is a godsend when you need it for research for something or someone, and after reading about Bob's NFL career and his coaching life, I finally found a link for him at the New York State Department of Labor. I quickly dialed the number. Would he remember me after so many years?

It took me a while before I was able to locate his department. And when I finally got through to the right office asking to speak to Bob Taylor, the voice on the other end of the line said, "Mister Taylor no longer works here."

That wasn't exactly the answer I was hoping for. "Did he retire? Move to a different department?" I asked.

The voice said, "I don't believe so."

I told the person on the other end that I was an old friend of Bob's, and it was important that I reach him. I then asked if he could check with someone there to see if they knew where I could find him. I didn't want to sound too desperate, but I probably did. He put me on hold. When the person came back, he said, "You might try the Weill-Cornell Medical Center. That's all I can tell you," and he hung up.

I dialed the medical center number, and after being directed to several different extensions, the nurse who answered the phone said, "Mr. Taylor is not able to take any calls at this time. Just this morning, he came out of surgery. You'll have to wait until tomorrow to call."

I was up early the next morning, anxious as I dialed the hospital's number. After being transferred several times again, a solemn voice on the other end spoke. "Mister Taylor passed away last night. I'm sorry."

I was too late

I sat at my desk, numb. It took a damn speech to remember

how important Bob had been in my life, and now I had missed the opportunity to let him know in person. It wasn't that I did not want to respond to his letter back then. When I got that letter, I thought to myself, *Once I have some free time, I'll write him back or just call him.* The problem was the days turned into weeks, the weeks into months, the months into years . . . and I never did. I had kept that letter all those years, but my work, my family, and my life seemed to push my response to him as far back as the letter was in the drawer.

I think sometimes in our lives we let time go by without realizing that our journey has an end. And if we don't reach out to those people who were important in our lives, we may never get a chance to express gratitude for their friendship. As I looked up at the Maryland State College diploma hanging on the wall, I imagined seeing the face of a young Bob Taylor and I softly whispered the words, "Thank you."

2020 TIMELINE

January 17, 2020. The CDC began Covid–19 screenings of air travelers coming into the United States from China.

February 23, 2020. In Brunswick, Georgia, twenty-five-year-old Ahmaud Arbery was killed while out on a run after being followed and videotaped by a white man in a pickup truck.

March 13, 2020. In Louisville, Kentucky, twenty-six-year-old EMT Breonna Taylor was shot eight times and killed after police broke down the door to her apartment while executing a nighttime warrant.

May 25, 2020. In Minneapolis, Minnesota, forty-six-year-old George Floyd died after being handcuffed and pinned to the ground by police officer Derek Chauvin, with his knee on Floyd's neck.

May 26, 2020. Protestors in Minneapolis took to the streets to protest Floyd's killing. Police cars were set on fire and officers released tear gas to disperse crowds. After months of quarantine and isolation during a global pandemic, protests mounted, spreading across the country and around the world in the following days.

June 5, 2020. Washington, D.C.'s Mayor Muriel Boser had the words "BLACK LIVES MATTER" painted on 16th Street near the White House. The term "Black lives matter" was started in a July 2013 Facebook post, responding to the acquittal of George Zimmerman who shot and killed unarmed seventeen-year-old

Trayvon Martin on February 26, 2012 in Sanford, Florida. The movement would become the largest U.S. protest movement in 2020, with street paintings proclaiming these three words throughout American cities.

June 8, 2020. The National Bureau of Economic Research officially declared that the U.S. was in a recession, with over 22 million jobs lost.

June 12, 2020. In Atlanta, Georgia, Rayshard Brooks, a twenty-seven-year-old African-American man, was fatally shot by an Atlanta Police Department officer. His crime: Falling asleep in his car at a fast-food restaurant drive-through.

August 17–20, 2020. The Democratic National Convention, based at the Wisconsin Center in Milwaukee and attended by speakers virtually from around the United States, nominated Joseph Biden as their Presidential Candidate for 2020. Previously, Mr. Biden announced his choice as his Vice Presidential running mate. Kamala Harris, of Jamaican and Asian descent, became the first woman of color in history to hold the honor as candidate for the office.

August 23, 2020. In Kenosha, Wisconsin, Jacob S. Blake, a twenty-nine-year-old Black man, was shot from behind seven times by a police officer. Police were attempting to arrest Blake amid a domestic dispute, during which Blake was tased and scuffled briefly with officers. He was shot as he tried to enter his SUV, where his children were in the back seat.

Epilogue

Looking back at my days at Maryland State College, it is important to recognize some of the people who played major roles in my life, as well as those whom I came to admire as they moved forward with their own lives.

If it were not for Coach Watson's interview that I heard on the radio so many years ago, I really don't know where I would be today. That interview led me to enroll in a college that I hardly knew existed; a college that changed my life forever. Little did I know as I listened to the interview that Coach "Pop" Watson, head of the Physical Education department at Maryland State College, would be the guiding light in my chosen field. I also had the privilege of meeting Coach Vernon "Skip" McCain, a truly outstanding leader, educator, and of course, football coach. He served as Maryland State College's head football coach from 1948 to 1963, a period of fifteen years in which he became the most successful African-American head coach in college football history—a record which still stands today.

In just my two years at Maryland, I saw several of our school's football players go on to have illustrious careers in professional football. They included Emerson Boozer, Earl Christy—and, of course, Bob Taylor.

Graduating in 1965, Emerson Boozer was drafted by the New York Jets and went on to win All-Pro honors, an American Football League championship, and he played in Super Bowl III. His entire career was spent with the Jets, where he was Joe Namath's primary blocker in the memorable Super Bowl III championship, winning the game from the favored Baltimore Colts. Inducted into the College Football Hall of Fame in 2010, Boozer led an illustrious career and won honors throughout his nine-year football career.

Earl Christy was the ultimate sportsman who excelled in track and field, basketball, and football. He was a Dean's List student, and I was privileged to be in classes with Christy as we both majored in Physical Education. Graduating in 1966, Christy was drafted by the New York Jets. He became one of the five Maryland State College Hawks alumni to play in the 1968 Super Bowl game, along with Emerson Boozer, Johnny Sample, Charlie Stukes, and Jim Duncan.

While Bob Taylor may have preferred playing golf, he made his name on the football field. Drafted by the New York Giants in 1963, he was traded in 1965 to the Minnesota Vikings before moving on to the Winnipeg Blue Bombers of the Canadian Football League. He returned to the University of Maryland Eastern Shore as head football coach in 1969.

Perhaps the most noted of all Maryland State College football standouts was Art Shell. He was drafted by the Oakland Raiders in 1968. Shell's career took him from winning two Super Bowl Championships, to the head coaching job for the Raiders in 1989, the first Black head coach in modern National Football League history. He ultimately became the NFL's Senior Vice President for Operations and Development.

Dr. William Hytche, Sr., the Algebra instructor who taught me to see numbers and letters in a new light, went on to serve as President of the University of Maryland Eastern Shore for two decades. Under Dr. Hytche's leadership, the school more than tripled its enrollment from 1,046 when he took control of the school in 1975 to 3,209 students in 1997. About 32 academic programs were added during his tenure.

As for myself, after two years of life-changing experiences on the Maryland State College campus, I departed with a degree in hand, no money in my pockets, and all sorts of hopes and dreams rattling around in my head. But I certainly never could have predicted the direction my life would veer in, or the opportunities I would have to change lives through sports that still amaze me when thinking about them all these years later. During those early post-graduation years my career took on a life of its own, with opportunities I'd never thought would come my way. I taught Physical Education for several years in Delaware and it ultimately led to my landing the position of National Director of Youth Sports with the Chicago-based Athletic Institute in 1973. During that time, I convened, for the first time ever, the leaders of all of America's top youth sports organizations to discuss the issues of parental and coaches' behavior in children's sports.

But my most important job was being a father. I didn't take Bob's advice, and Mike and I went on to have seven children. And it was through watching their experiences on fields and courts in the various communities we lived in that I recognized a common problem that was surfacing: parents were volunteering to coach their children's teams, but so many of them were going about it the wrong way. They had wonderful intentions and were giving freely of their time to work with children–but no one had ever told them how to do it. Many chose to coach like the professional and college coaches they saw on television, which translated into a lot of yelling and demeaning of youngsters when the team failed to win that day. Kids were being traumatized and chased away from sports they loved.

The unintentional abuse they suffered, both emotional and physical, took a toll and had major ramifications on their lives moving forward. Research showed that, by the age of thirteen, 70 percent of children who began playing sports as young as five years old would drop out. I had experienced a coach's abuse when growing up and then watched it happen in my household when my kids played for coaches who directed demeaning comments at them.

The abhorrent behavior of coaches and parents touched a nerve in me, and an idea began to emerge. I would create a training program for coaches to undergo before stepping onto the field with children. Coaches would be trained not only in sports, but in the psychology of the child's mind as he or she navigated their way through the different sports being offered. It was a novel idea, but a necessary one.

As I forged ahead, I encountered rejection from youth organizations who feared coaches would no longer volunteer. But I believed with all my heart that it would take hold, and I refused to give up—and in 1981, I created the National Youth Sports Coaches Association (NYSCA). Coaches gathered in meeting rooms at parks and recreation departments and watched a video played on a VCR that I had put together featuring insight from experts on topics such as the psychology of coaching and safety, among many other areas. Gradually, as more recreation agencies learned about the program, they came on board and began utilizing the training for their volunteers.

By the early 1990s, NYSCA had become enormously successful and evolved into the National Alliance for Youth Sports (NAYS). The training became the most widely used program in the country for independent youth leagues, YMCAs/YWCAs, church programs, Boys & Girls Clubs, and the list goes on. Plus, it has meant so much to work with our beloved U.S. Military bases worldwide that offer youth sports programming. These are the amazing men and women who protect our freedoms while risking their lives; and so many of them somehow find time in their schedules to work with children in sports.

It continues to give me enormous pride to still be a part of these efforts and to know all the good that is being done for kids of all colors, ethnicities, and genders—all through the incredible power of sports. Sports changed my life and I love seeing its impact on kids. NAYS has never wavered from its focus of helping to ensure that children have safe, positive, and rewarding experiences in sports, and to level the playing ground for all children to have equal opportunities on the fields and courts of their communities. I am forever grateful to all the incredible recreation professionals who are devoted to making a difference in the lives of children through the power of sports in their communities. Especially, to those that have utilized NAYS training programs and resources to help them in their endeavors.

I have often wondered what path my life would have taken if I had not attended an all-Black college in 1961. I had grown up in a time when signs on bathrooms and water fountains were marked "Whites Only." When Black families were prohibited from going to "white" beaches and were only allowed to sit in the balcony sections of movie theaters. When Jim Crow laws enforced segregation in schools, housing, and at work—these were only some of the more obvious signs of racism that existed in our country.

What was less obvious was the poverty forced on these racially divided communities. The name calling, the unfair justice system, and the generational attitude that whites were somehow superior prevailed. I saw the behavior of my parents when it came to dealing with people of color, and I said nothing. I saw it all around me, and I said nothing. And while I may have been friends with the two Black musicians in my brother's band, I simply accepted the status quo. I was like too many people growing up in this country, not questioning this injustice. And when I decided to go to a segregated college, I did it so I could get ahead in my life, not to break any sort of barriers. What I did not expect to see was how my attitude of doing nothing was no better than overt racism—and that was an education that has shaped the direction of my life ever since.

Just one year after my graduation, in July 1964, the Federal government passed the Civil Rights Act, which prohibited segregation in public places and banned discrimination based on race, color, religion, sex, or national origin. Certainly all worthy objectives, but the reality of our society today is that they were simply words on paper. None of these goals have been met. Racism—whether apparent or concealed—is a difficult behavior to overcome. Unfortunately, it's generational. Racism will only become a thing of the past if we teach future generations not to hate others simply because they are different. We still have a long way to go, but it can be done. My relationship with Bob Taylor is only one example—*my* example—that shows that it is possible.

About Fred Engh and Jann Seal

Fred Engh has been involved in youth sports for over forty years—as a coach, athletic director, and sports educator. In 1971, he became the National Director of youth sports for the Athletic Institute in Chicago. While at the Institute, he was promoted to Executive Director. In 1981, Fred founded a national program dedicated to the training and certification of volunteer coaches—a program that has now trained over three million coaches. This group has evolved into the National Alliance for Youth Sports, a nonprofit organization that works to provide safe and fun sports for America's youth.

As the former president of the Alliance, Fred Engh has been a featured speaker in over 200 cities throughout the world. He has also appeared on CNN and on numerous television shows, including *Dateline NBC* and ABC's *20/20*. Currently, Fred resides in West Palm Beach, Florida, with his wife, Michaele.

Jann Briggs Goodman Hiller Seal attended the University of Maryland in College Park receiving her undergraduate degree in English. After driving around the world in a Land Rover and writing about her adventures, she began her career teaching high school English in Baltimore's inner city. With a move to Los Angeles, she became an advertising copy writer opening the door to writing for network television soap operas. Jann currently writes and edits magazines and newspaper articles and has published a cookbook. She and her husband Paul live in Lake Worth, Florida.

The National Alliance
for Youth Sports
BOOK SERIES

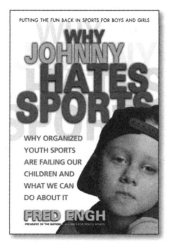

Why Johnny Hates Sports

Why Organized Youth Sports Are Failing Our Children and What We Can Do About It

Fred Engh

Mom! Do I really have to go to the game? Can't I just stay home?" All across this country, an ever-increasing number of children are dropping out of organized sports—soccer, baseball, football, swimming, and more—not because they don't like to play, but because the system they play in is failing them. Written by one of this country's leading advocates of children's sports, *Why Johnny Hates Sports* is the first book to look at the growing problems inherent in the way we introduce our children to sports.

In this timely book, Fred Engh examines the unsettling state of youth sports in America. He explains how and why many of the original goals of the youth leagues have been affected by today's win-at-all-costs attitude. He then documents the negative physical and psychological impact that parents, coaches, and administrators can have on children. Most important, he provides a wide variety of proven solutions to each and every one of the problems covered. Throughout the book, Engh relates stories drawn from hundreds of real-life experiences.

Why Johnny Hates Sports is both an exposé of abuses and a call to arms. It clearly shows us a serious problem that has been going on too long—a problem that, until now, has been tolerated by most, with little concern for its effect on our children. It also provides practical answers that can alter the destructive course that youth sports have taken.

About the Author

Fred Engh has been involved in youth sports for over thirty years—as a coach, athletic director, and sports educator. In 1971, he became the National Director of youth sports for the Athletic Institute in Chicago. While at the Institute, he was promoted to Executive Director. In 1981, Fred founded a national program dedicated to the training and certification of volunteer coaches—a program that has now trained over three million coaches. This group has evolved into the National Alliance for Youth Sports, a nonprofit organization that works to provide safe and fun sports for America's youth.

$14.95 • 224 pages • ISBN 978-0-7570-0041-6

Your First Coaching Book

A Practical Guide for Volunteer Coaches

The National Alliance for Youth Sports

For the millions of children involved in youth sports, it is their coach who plays a major role in the way they will feel about playing. It is the coach who is entrusted with the tasks of organizing the team, setting up training activities, managing the game, handling medical crises, and buying the post-game pizzas. Unfortunately, few youth sports organizations provide any real training for their coaches. Instead, those who volunteer for this job must pick up the information on their own or learn it as they go. The result of this inexperience can be seen in the increasingly large percentage of kids who drop out of organized leagues.

To help coaches understand their important role, including the challenges that lie ahead of them, the National Alliance for Youth Sports—America's premier youth sports advocacy group—has created a simple and straightforward guide for coaches. It presents the factors that make up good coaching, the tasks a coach is responsible for, and how a coach can best deal with the most common problems faced both on and off the playing field. Solidly based on the Alliance's twenty-five years of experience with youth sports organizations, Your First Coaching Book offers sound and practical advice on all key issues.

About The National Alliance for Youth Sports

The *National Alliance for Youth Sports* is America's leading advocate for positive and safe sports for children. The Alliance features a wide range of programs that educate volunteer coaches, parents, youth sport program administrators, and officials about their roles and responsibilities in the context of youth sports. It also offers youth development programs for children. The Alliance's programs are provided at the local level through dynamic partnerships with more than 2,400 community-based organizations, such as parks and recreation departments, Boys and Girls Clubs, Police Athletic Leagues, YMCA/YWCAs, and other independent youth service groups throughout the country, as well as military installations worldwide.

$4.95 • 64 pages • ISBN 978-0-7570-0200-2

Secrets of Successful Coaching

Winning Tips & Advice from Fifty of America's Most Successful Coaches

Greg Bach

Coaching a youth sports team is as challenging as ever these days. Whether it's a T-ball team with 5- and 6-year-olds, an under-10 soccer team, or a travel basketball team with a roster of experienced players, coaches face a lengthy and imposing to-do list. Among the responsibilities are teaching skills, organizing productive practices, managing game days, instilling life lessons, and—most important of all—meeting the diverse needs of every child who is counting on you to make the season a memorable one for all the right reasons.

As you embark on your journey, who better to help you navigate the twists and turns that accompany a youth sports season than some of the most respected professional and collegiate coaches around—Joe Maddon, Karch Kiraly, Jenny Boucek, John Harbaugh, Ken Hitchcock, Charlotte Smith, and Sean Payton among others—who share incredible insights and wisdom in *Secrets of Successful Coaching*. Some of these coaches have reached the pinnacle of their sport, leading teams to Super Bowl titles and NCAA Championships; others have played under the bright lights and suffocating pressure of huge games before moving to the sidelines; and all possess that special touch when it comes to making a difference through the power of sports. They know the secrets to connecting with kids and the best ways of inspiring and motivating them, building their confidence, helping them learn from setbacks and disappointments, and what it takes to be a great leader and role model.

About the Author

Greg Bach, Senior Director of Communications for the National Alliance for Youth Sports,has had the good fortune to interview the country's most respected professional and collegiate coaches and athletes—as well as many leading experts in a variety of fields pertaining to youth sports. He is the author of eight books, including *Your First Coaching Book, A Parent's Guide to Baseball and Softball, Coaching Basketball for Dummies,* and *Coaching Soccer for Dummies.* A proud graduate of Michigan State University, where he majored in Journalism, he now resides in West Palm Beach, Florida.

$17.95 • 240 pages • ISBN 978-0-7570-0468-1

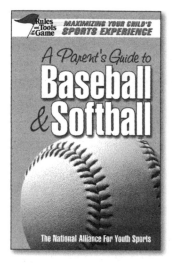

A Parent's Guide to Baseball & Softball

Maximizing Your Child's Sports Experience

The National Alliance for Youth Sports

Millions of kids throughout the country participate in organized youth programs each year. It's an exciting world of colorful uniforms, post-game ice cream treats, and lots of smiling faces. It's also one in which you as a parent can make a positive difference in helping your youngster grow and make the most of this experience. The *Rules & Tools of the Game Series* is here to lend a hand. Within each of the five books in this series, you will find a wealth of useful advice to help your child:

- Set and meet goals for the season.
- Develop the necessary skills for enjoyment of the sport.
- Build confidence and self-esteem.
- Display proper behavior and good sportsmanship at all times.
- Strive always to do his or her best.
- Effectively deal with disappointments, conflicts, and other challenges.
- Respect coaches, teammates, and opposing players.
- Prevent injuries through safety measures.

No matter what their age, children are going to remember this time forever. The *Rules & Tools of the Game Series* is an invaluable resource to help ensure that their memories are happy ones.

About The National Alliance for Youth Sports

The *National Alliance for Youth Sports* is America's leading advocate for positive and safe sports for children. The Alliance features a wide range of programs that educate volunteer coaches, parents, youth sport program administrators, and officials about their roles and responsibilities in the context of youth sports. It also offers youth development programs for children. The Alliance's programs are provided at the local level through dynamic partnerships with more than 2,400 community-based organizations, such as parks and recreation departments, Boys and Girls Clubs, Police Athletic Leagues, YMCA/YWCAs, and other independent youth service groups throughout the country, as well as military installations worldwide.

$4.95 • 64 pages • ISBN 978-0-7570-0204-5